FOR YOU ARE
ALL CHILDREN
OF
GOD THROUGH
FAITH IN
CHRIST JESUS
GALATIANS 3:26

SHE IS CLOTHED
WITH
STRENGTH AND
DIGNITY
PROVERBS 31:25

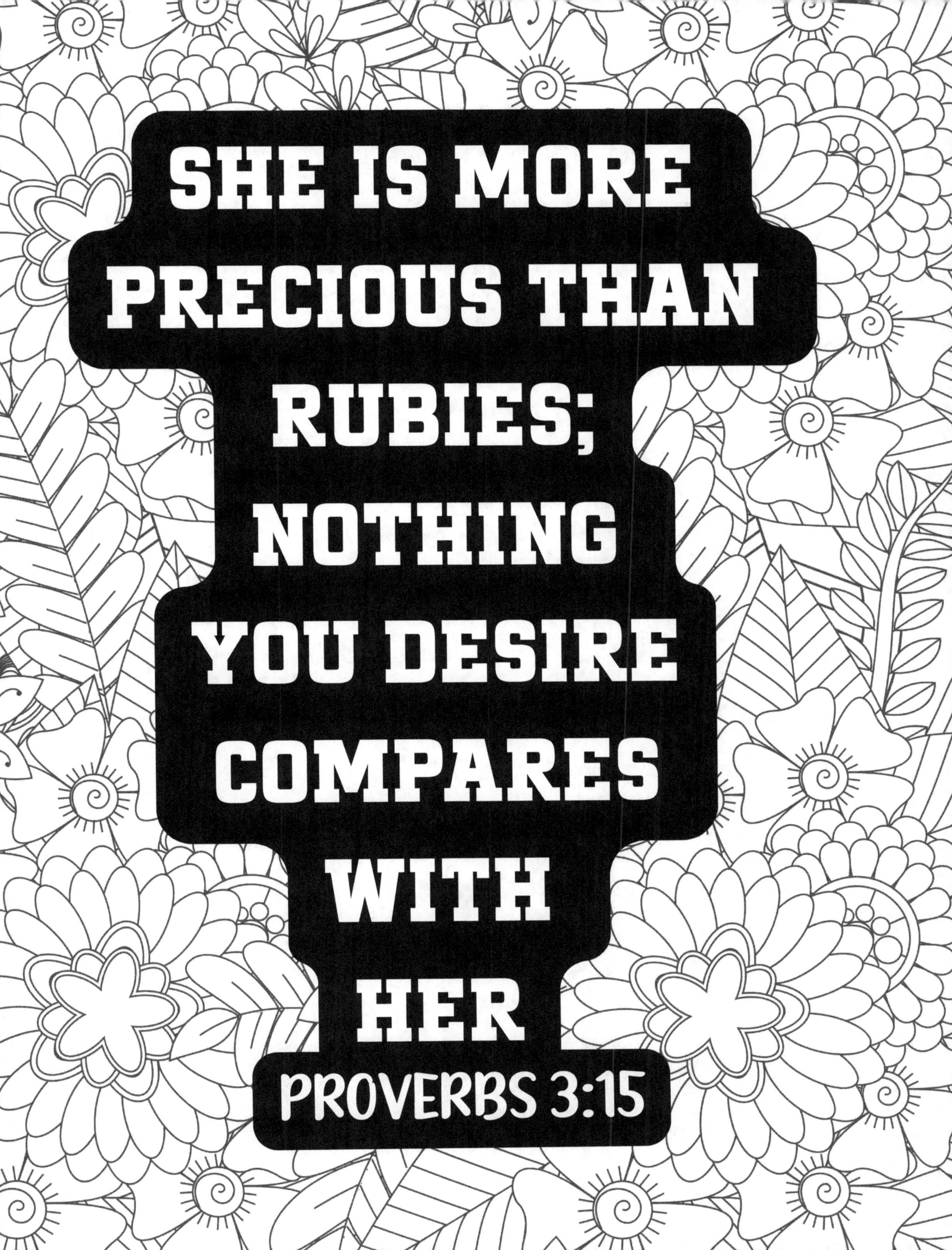

SHE IS MORE PRECIOUS THAN RUBIES; NOTHING YOU DESIRE COMPARES WITH HER
PROVERBS 3:15

SHE SPEAKS WITH WISDOM, & FAITHFUL INSTRUCTION IS ON HER TONGUE
PROVERBS 31:26

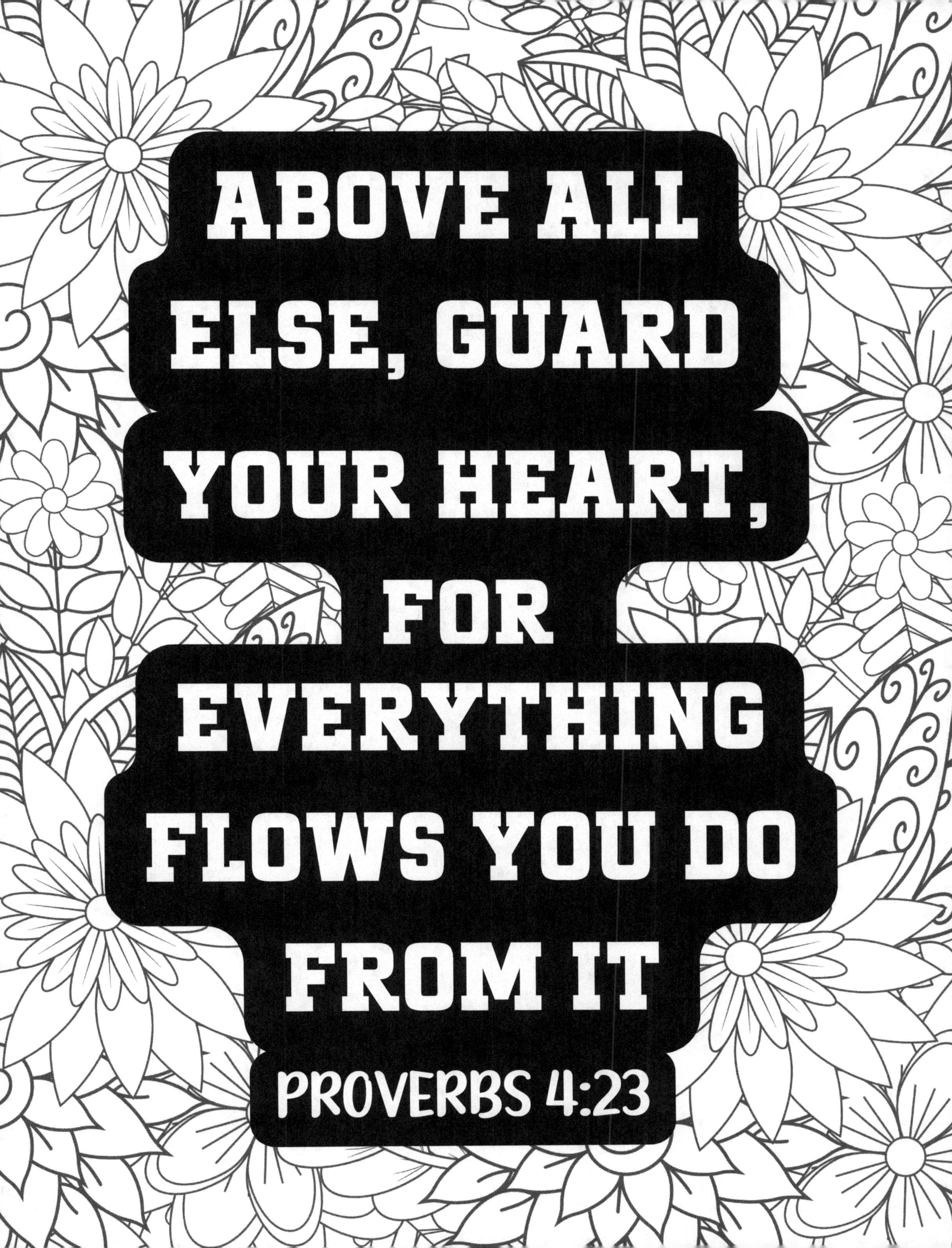

ABOVE ALL ELSE, GUARD YOUR HEART, FOR EVERYTHING FLOWS YOU DO FROM IT
PROVERBS 4:23

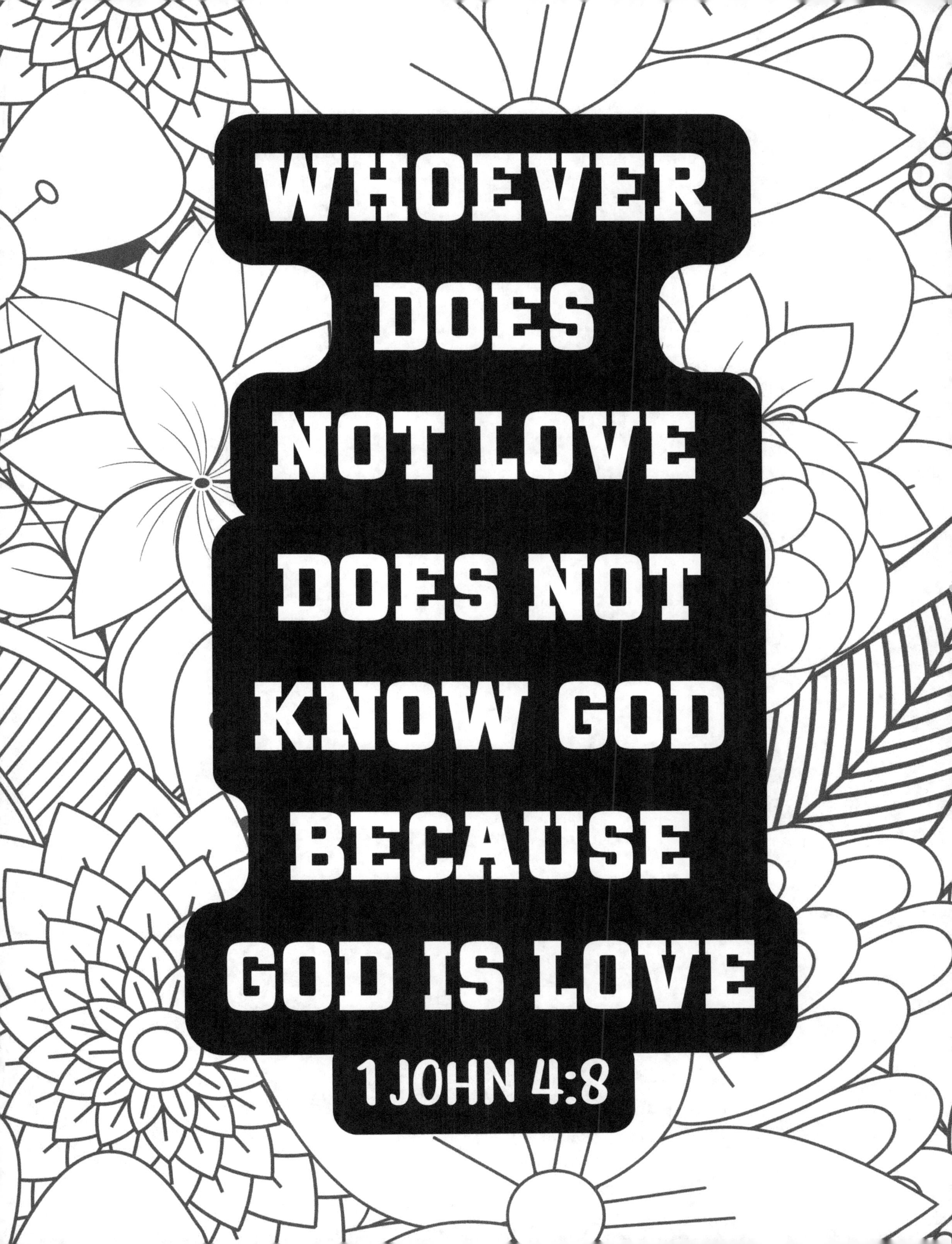

WHOEVER
DOES
NOT LOVE
DOES NOT
KNOW GOD
BECAUSE
GOD IS LOVE
1 JOHN 4:8

CLOTHE
YOURSELVES WITH
COMPASSION
KINDNESS
HUMILITY
GENTLENESS
& PATIENCE
COLOSSIANS 3:12

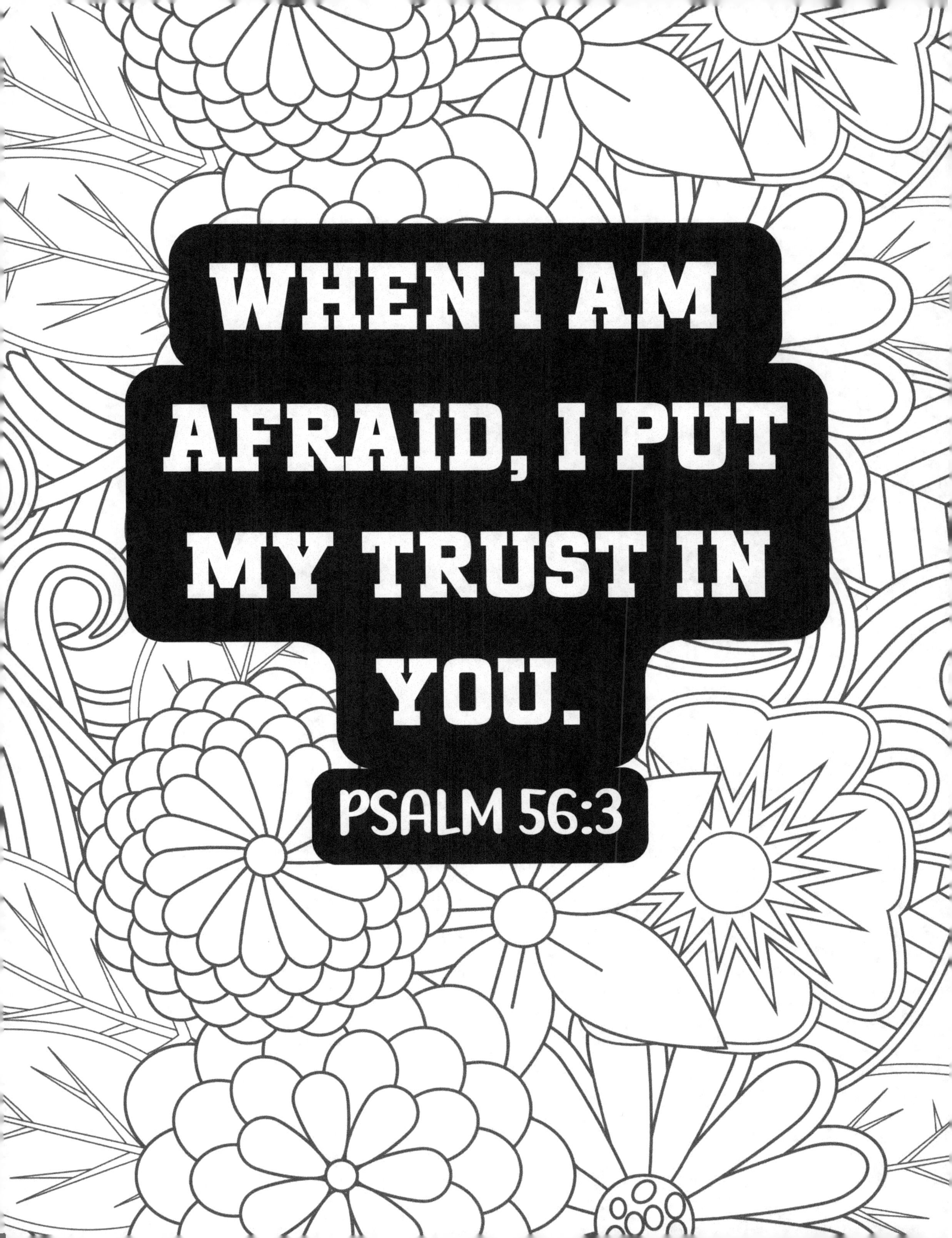

WHEN I AM AFRAID, I PUT MY TRUST IN YOU.
PSALM 56:3

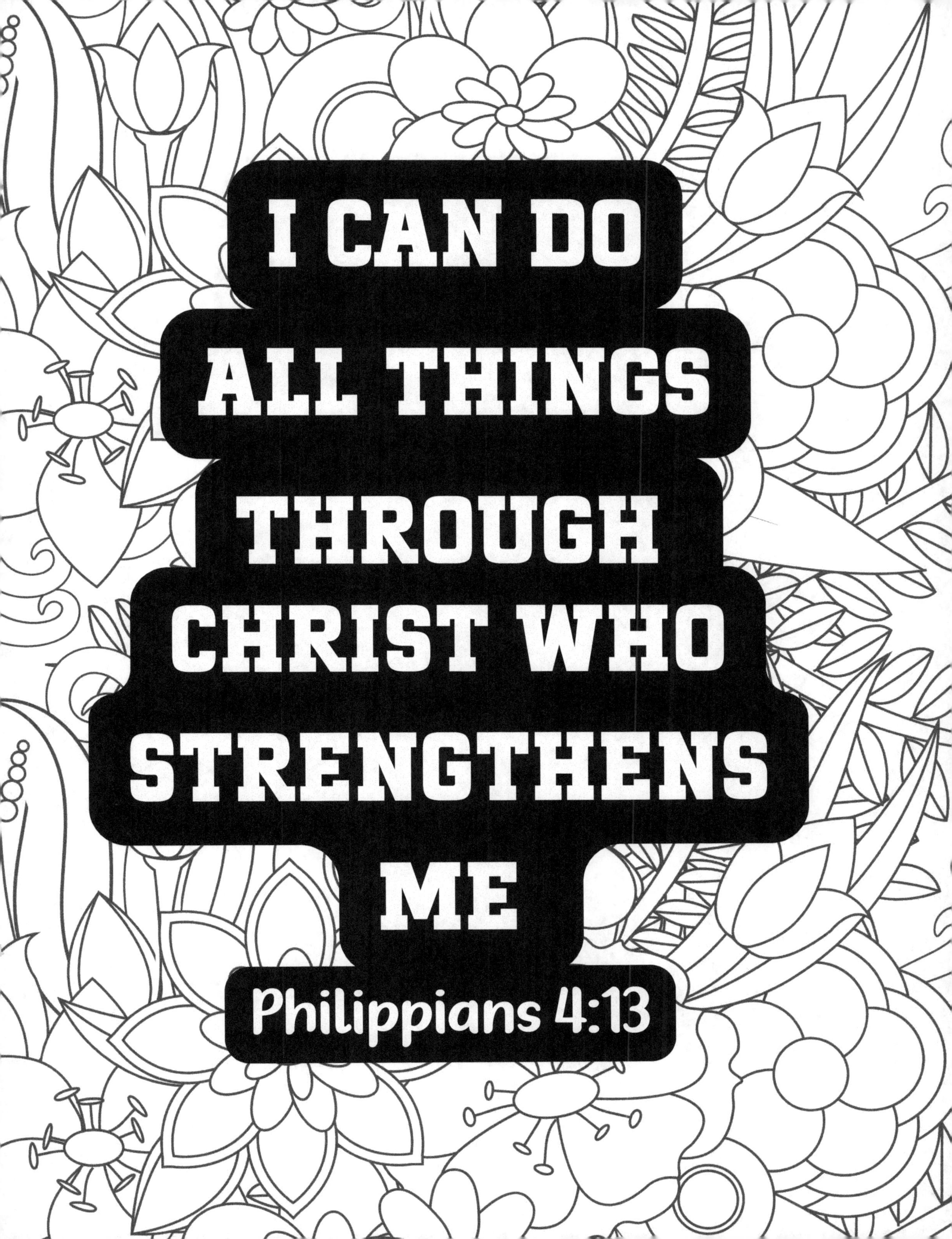

I CAN DO
ALL THINGS
THROUGH
CHRIST WHO
STRENGTHENS
ME
Philippians 4:13

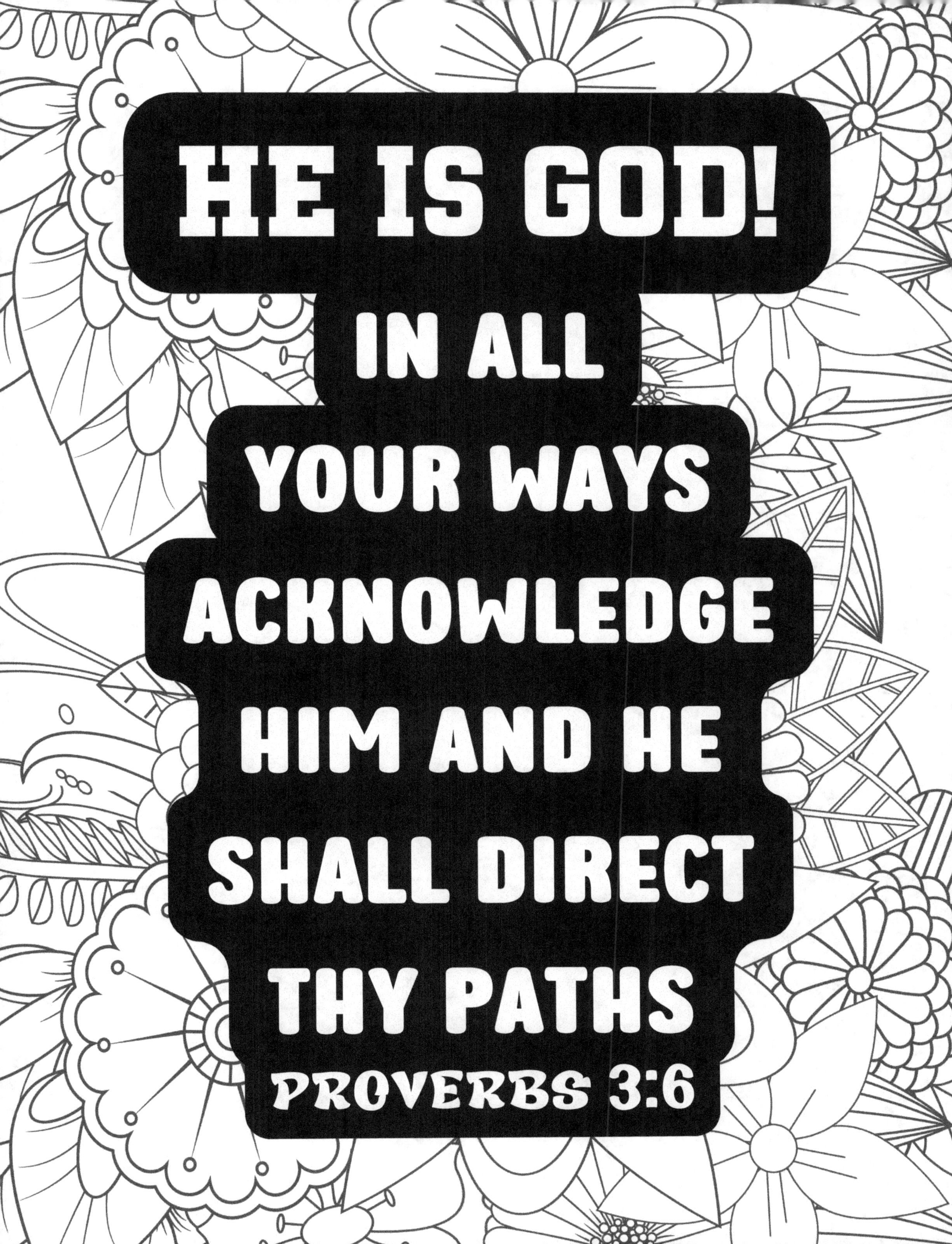

HE IS GOD!
IN ALL
YOUR WAYS
ACKNOWLEDGE
HIM AND HE
SHALL DIRECT
THY PATHS
PROVERBS 3:6

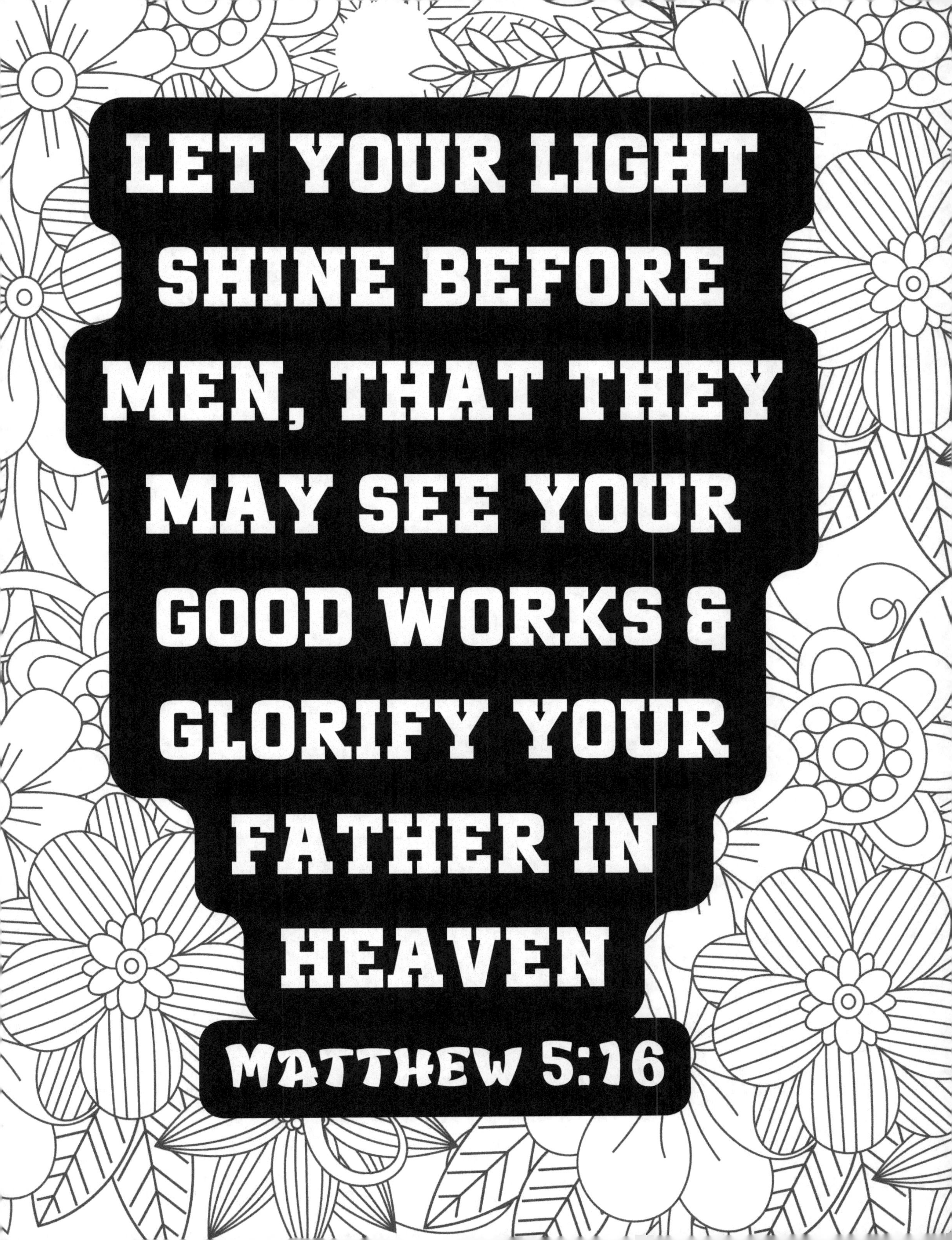

LET YOUR LIGHT SHINE BEFORE MEN, THAT THEY MAY SEE YOUR GOOD WORKS & GLORIFY YOUR FATHER IN HEAVEN
MATTHEW 5:16

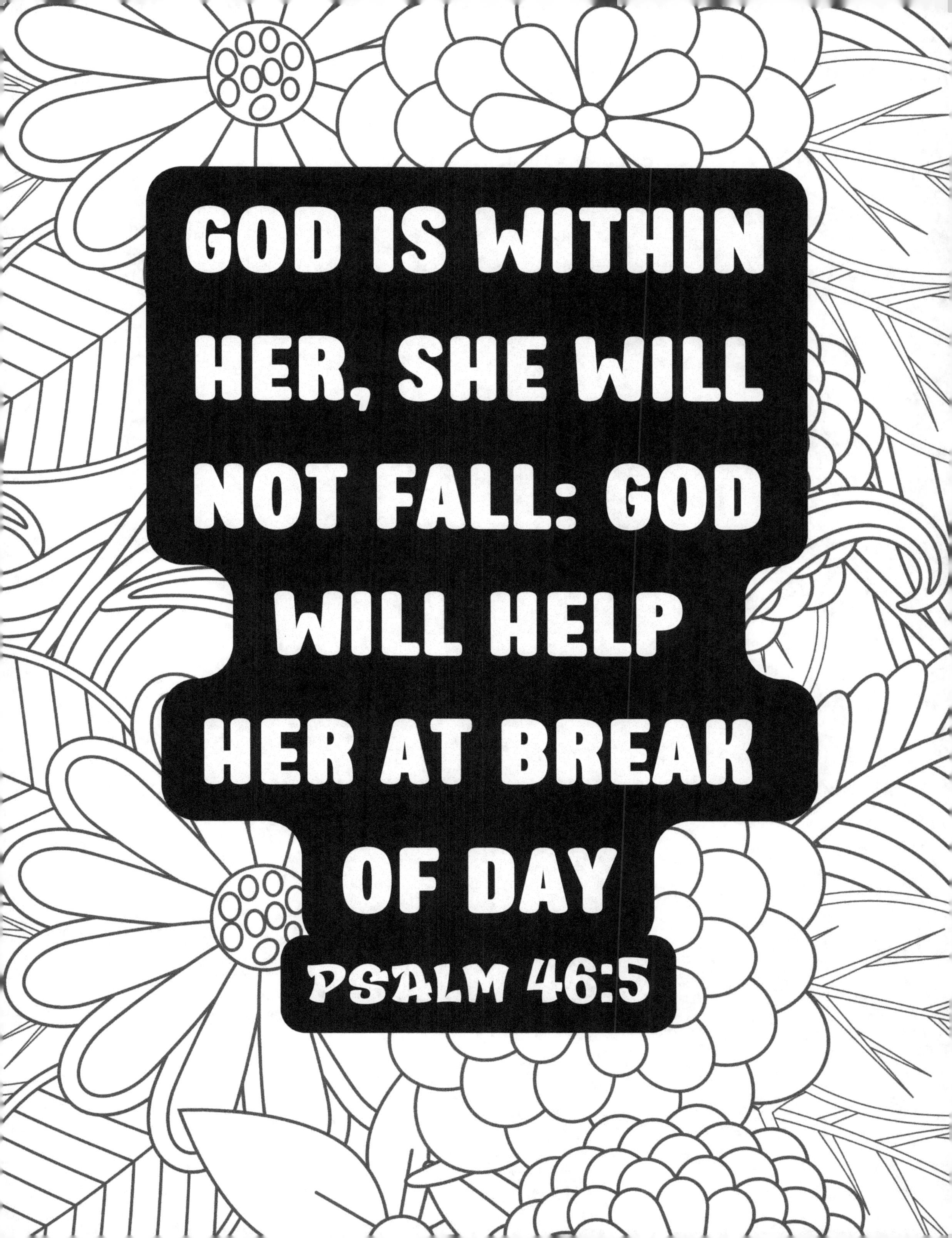

GOD IS WITHIN HER, SHE WILL NOT FALL: GOD WILL HELP HER AT BREAK OF DAY
PSALM 46:5

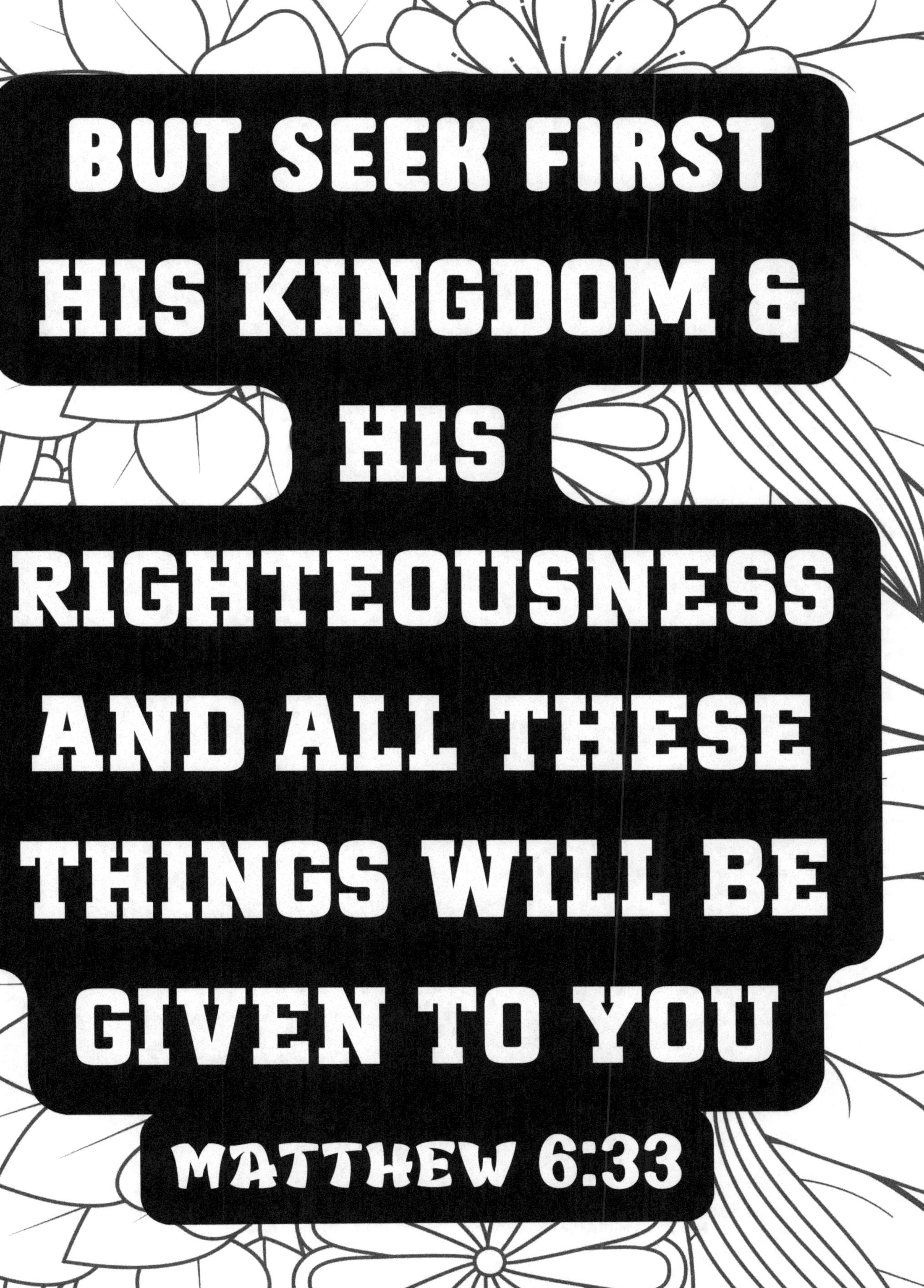

BUT SEEK FIRST HIS KINGDOM & HIS RIGHTEOUSNESS AND ALL THESE THINGS WILL BE GIVEN TO YOU
MATTHEW 6:33

AND MY GOD WILL MEET ALL YOUR NEEDS ACCORDING TO ALL HIS RICHES IN GLORY BY CHRIST JESUS
PHILIPPIANS 4:19

EVERY GOOD AND PERFECT GIFT IS FROM ABOVE...........
JAMES 1:17

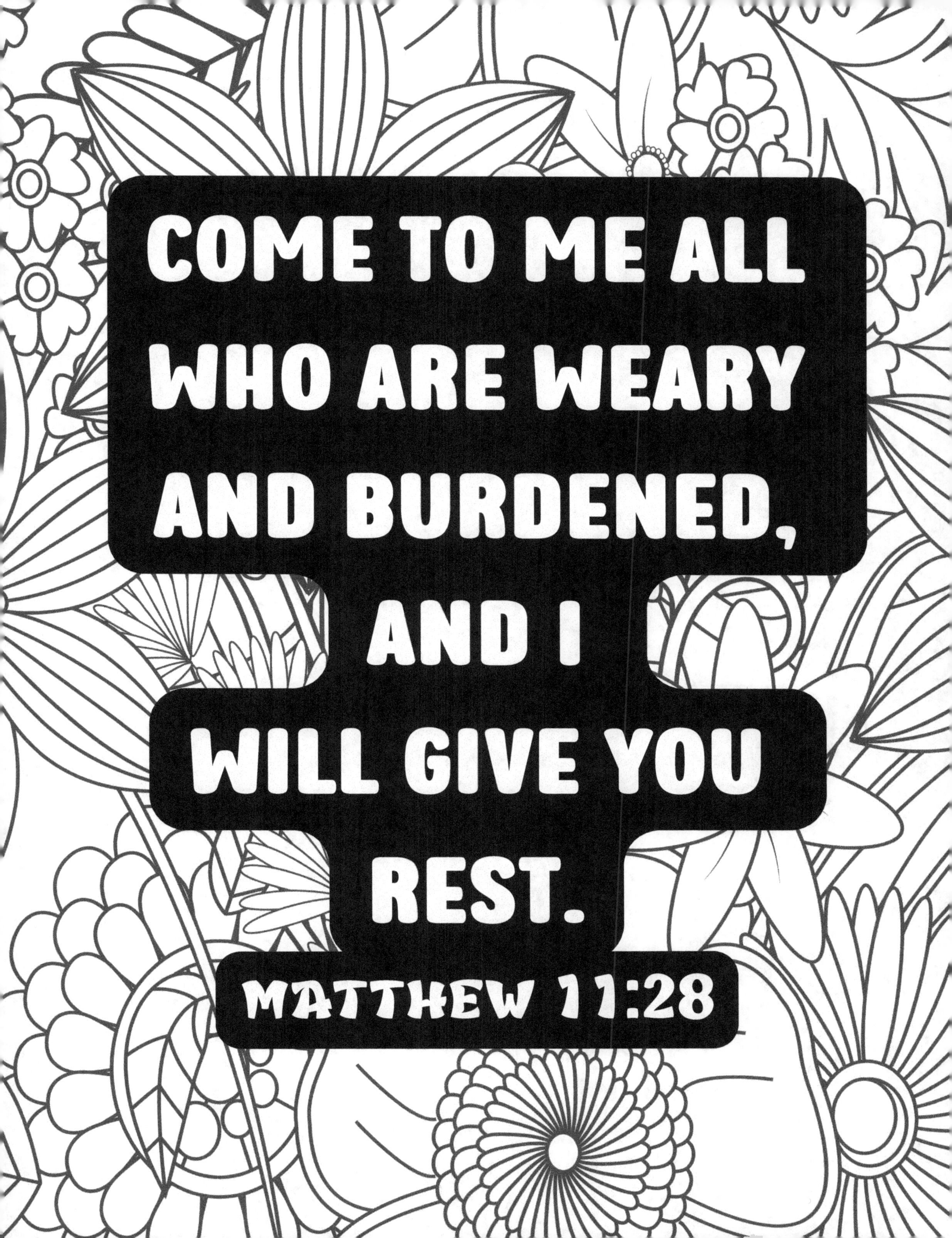

COME TO ME ALL WHO ARE WEARY AND BURDENED, AND I WILL GIVE YOU REST.
MATTHEW 11:28

FOR THE SPIRIT GOD GAVE US DOES NOT MAKE US TIMID, BUT GIVES US POWER, LOVE & A SOUND MIND
2 TIMOTHY 1:7

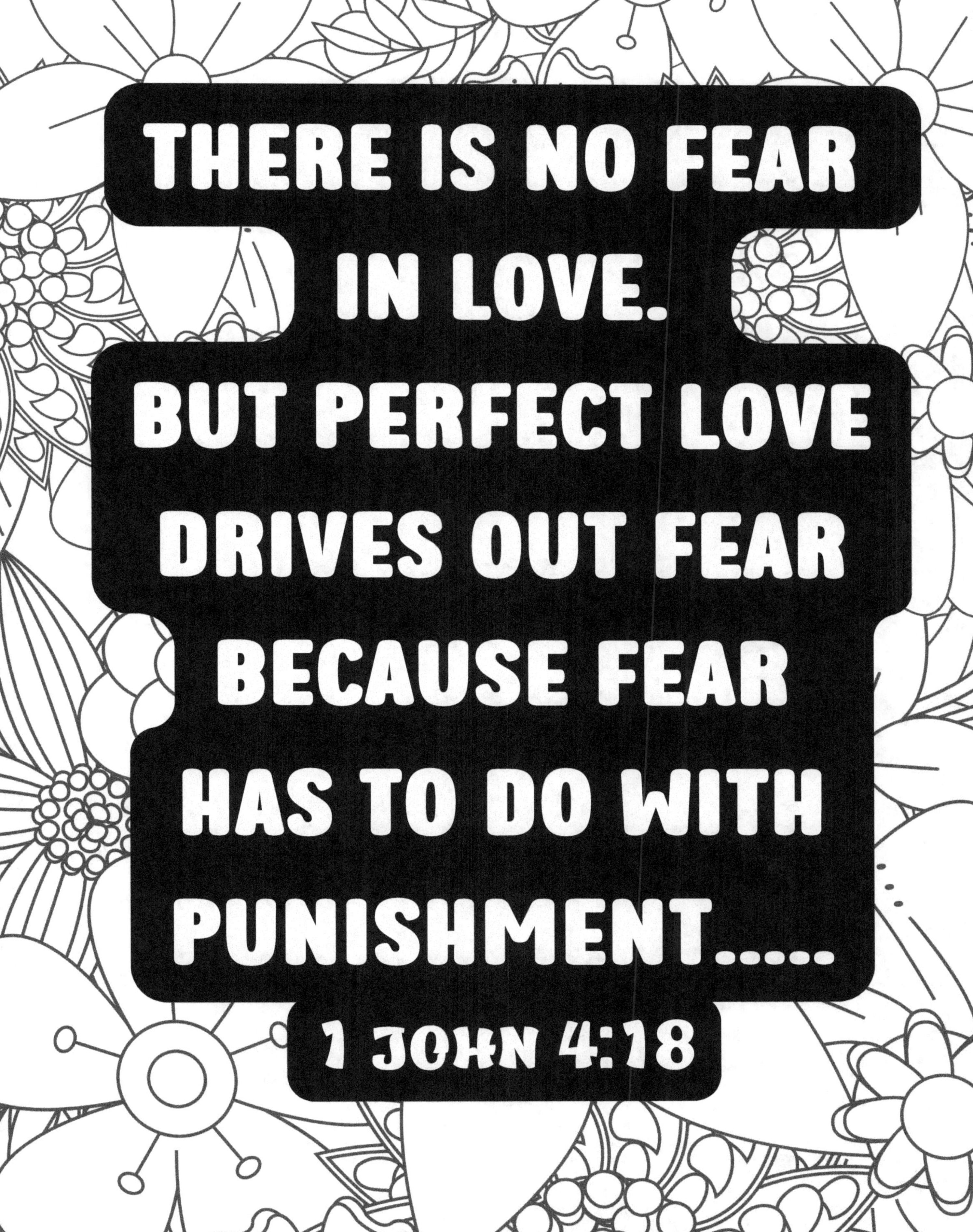

THERE IS NO FEAR
IN LOVE.
BUT PERFECT LOVE
DRIVES OUT FEAR
BECAUSE FEAR
HAS TO DO WITH
PUNISHMENT......
1 JOHN 4:18

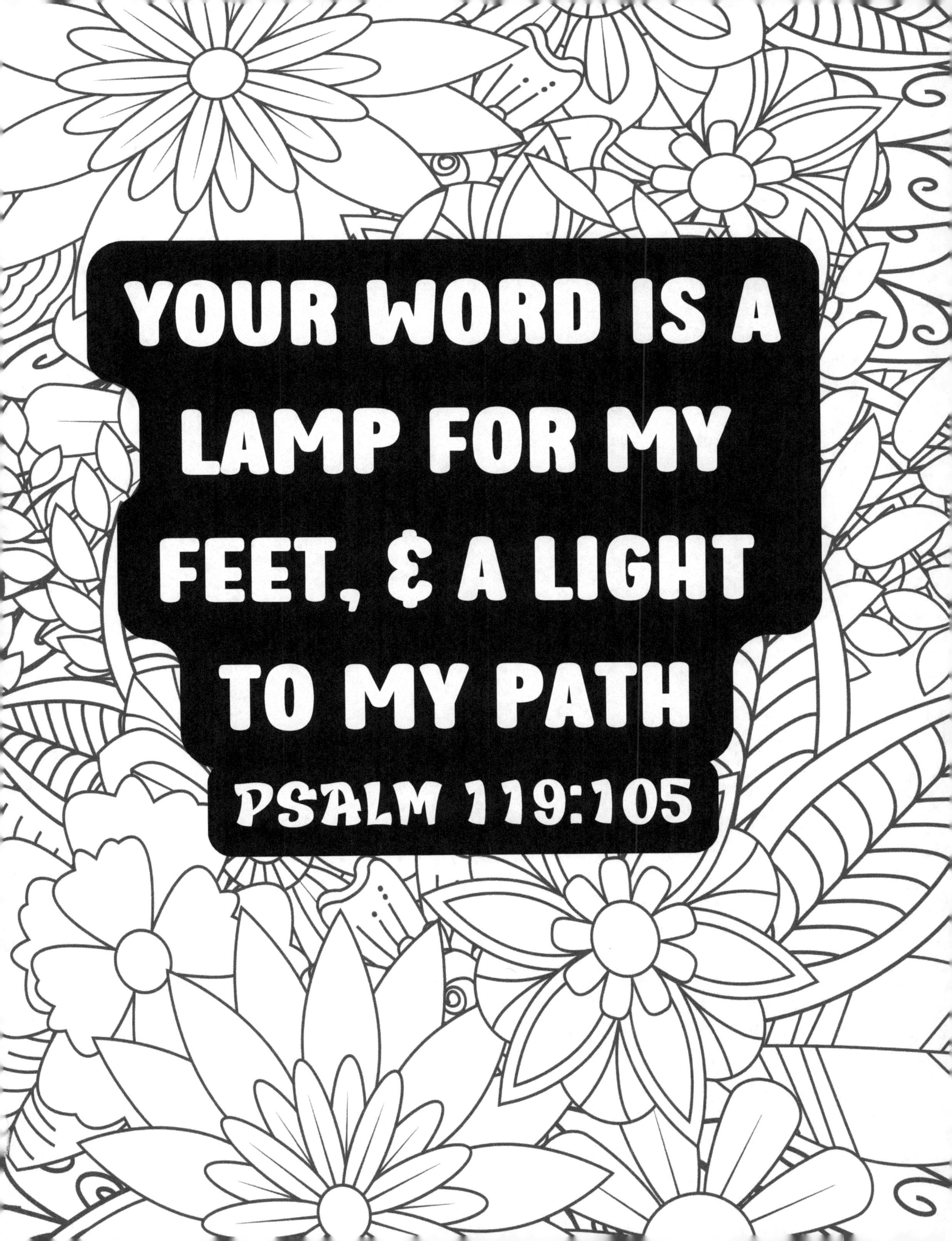

YOUR WORD IS A LAMP FOR MY FEET, & A LIGHT TO MY PATH
PSALM 119:105

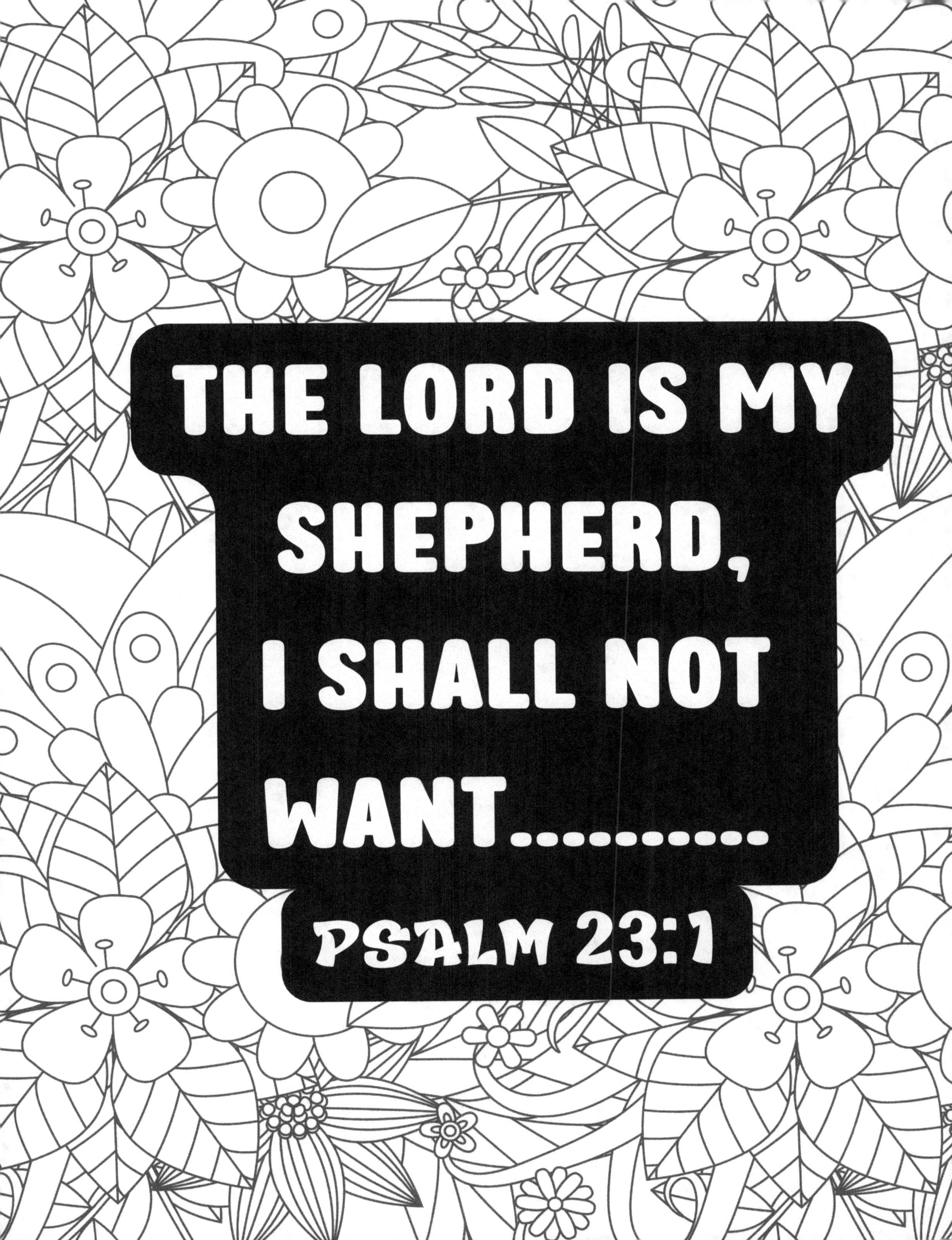
THE LORD IS MY SHEPHERD, I SHALL NOT WANT............
PSALM 23:1

BE JOYFUL IN HOPE, PATIENT IN AFFLICTION, FAITHFUL IN PRAYER
ROMANS 12:12

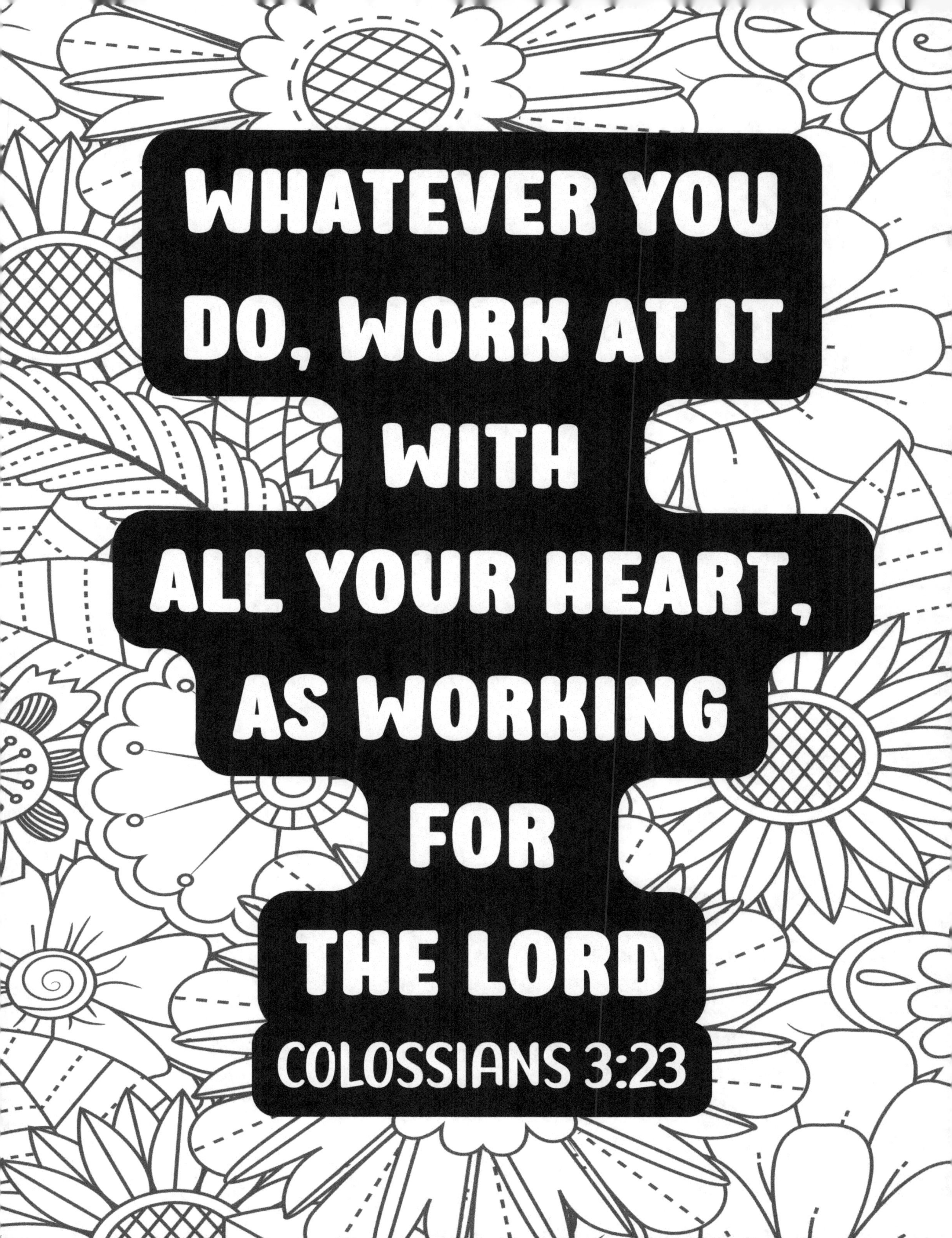

WHATEVER YOU DO, WORK AT IT WITH
ALL YOUR HEART, AS WORKING FOR
THE LORD
COLOSSIANS 3:23

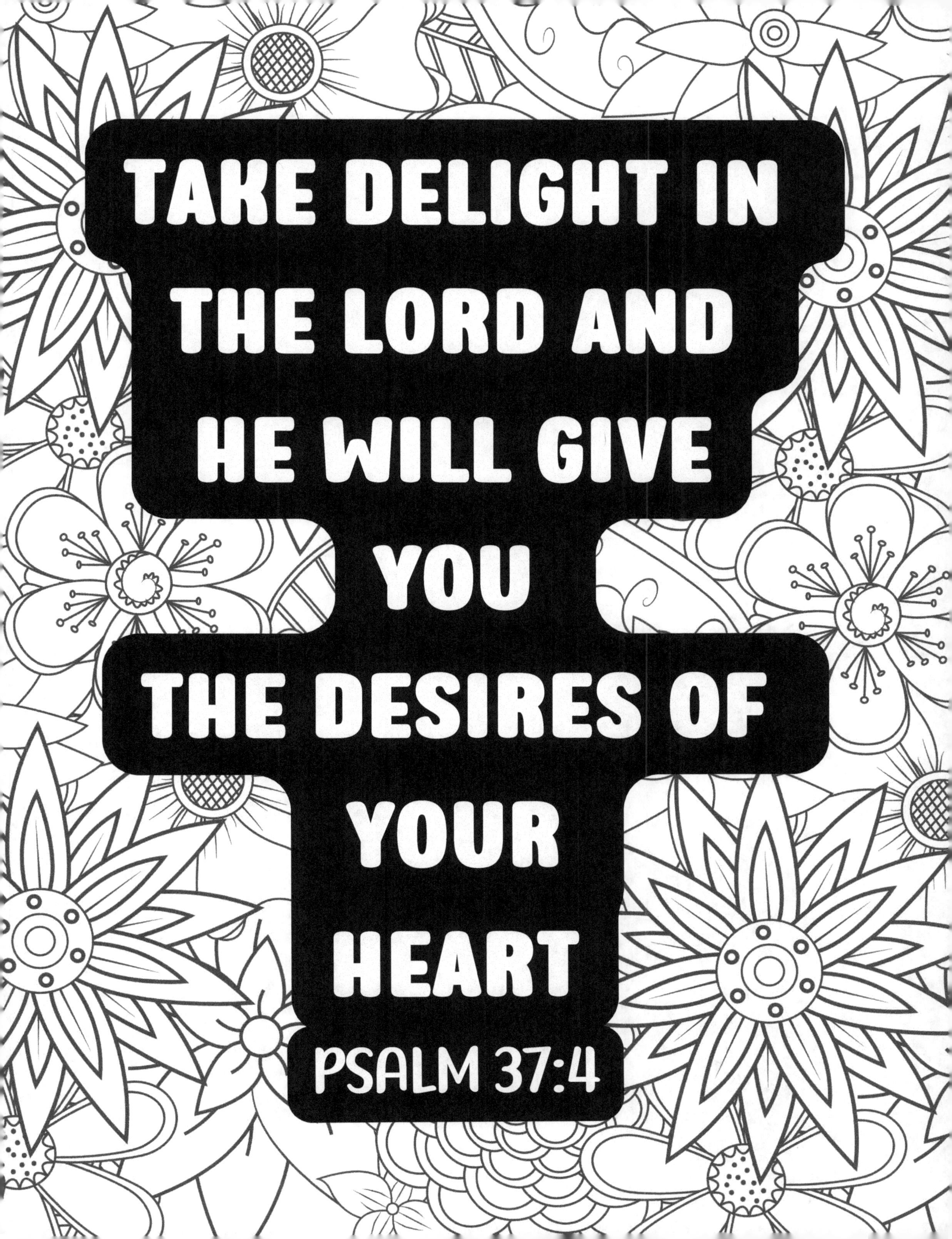

TAKE DELIGHT IN
THE LORD AND
HE WILL GIVE
YOU
THE DESIRES OF
YOUR
HEART
PSALM 37:4

BUT THE FRUIT OF THE SPIRIT IS LOVE, JOY, PEACE, KINDNESS, LONGSUFFERING, FAITHFULNESS, AND GOODNESS
GALATIANS 5:22

LET
EVERYTHING
YOU DO BE
IN LOVE.
1 CORINTHIANS 16:14

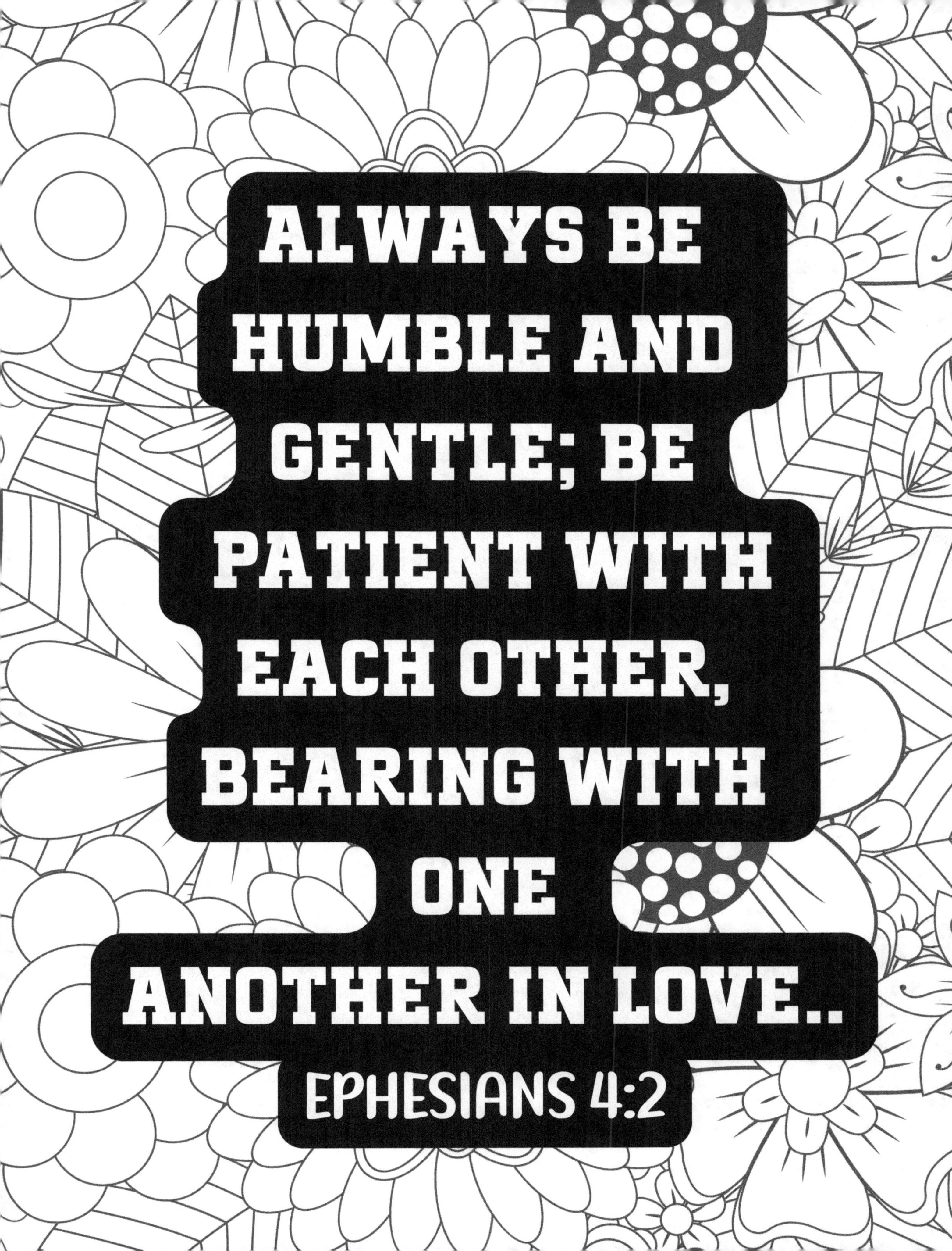

ALWAYS BE HUMBLE AND GENTLE; BE PATIENT WITH EACH OTHER, BEARING WITH ONE ANOTHER IN LOVE..
EPHESIANS 4:2

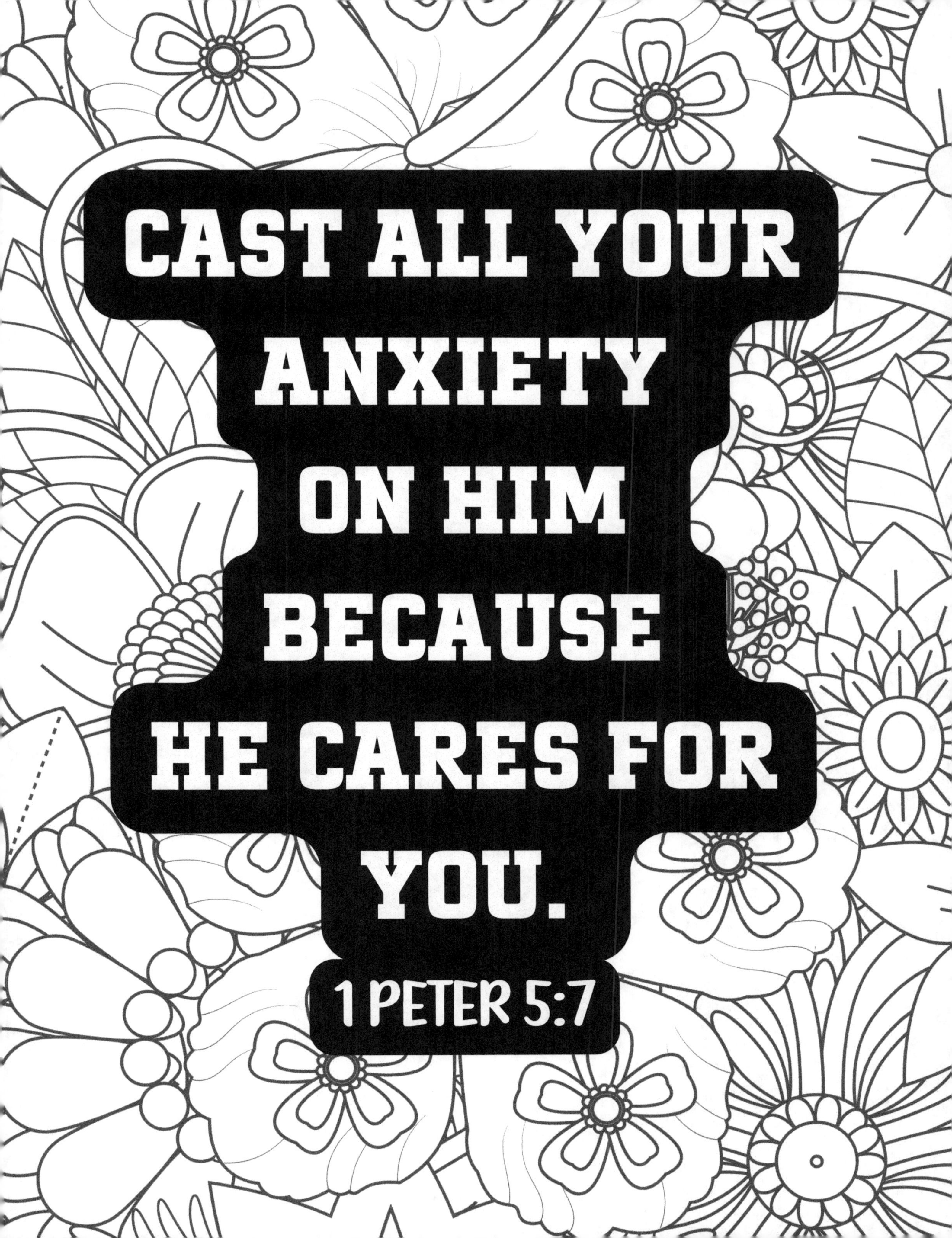

CAST ALL YOUR ANXIETY ON HIM BECAUSE HE CARES FOR YOU.
1 PETER 5:7

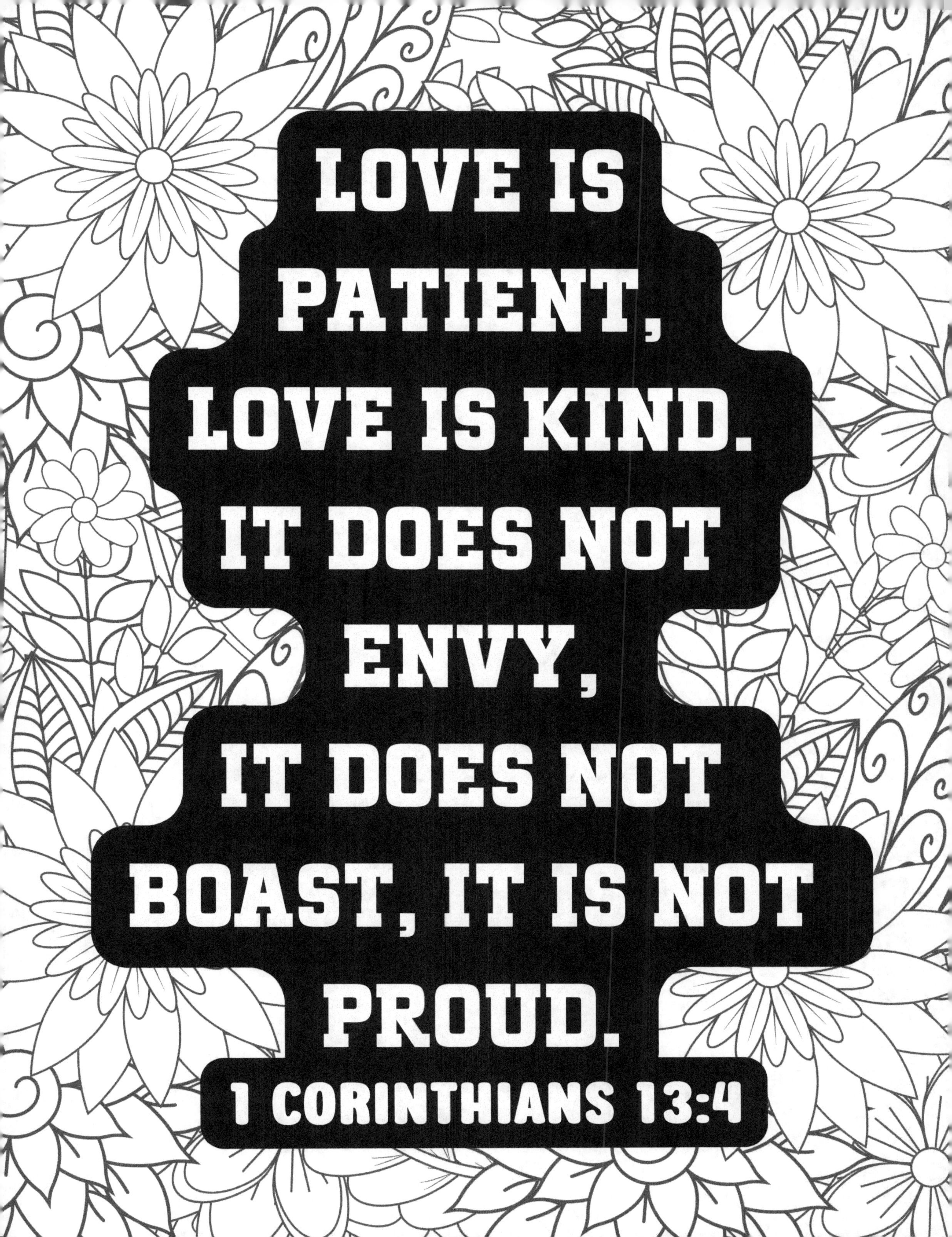

LOVE IS PATIENT, LOVE IS KIND. IT DOES NOT ENVY, IT DOES NOT BOAST, IT IS NOT PROUD.
1 CORINTHIANS 13:4

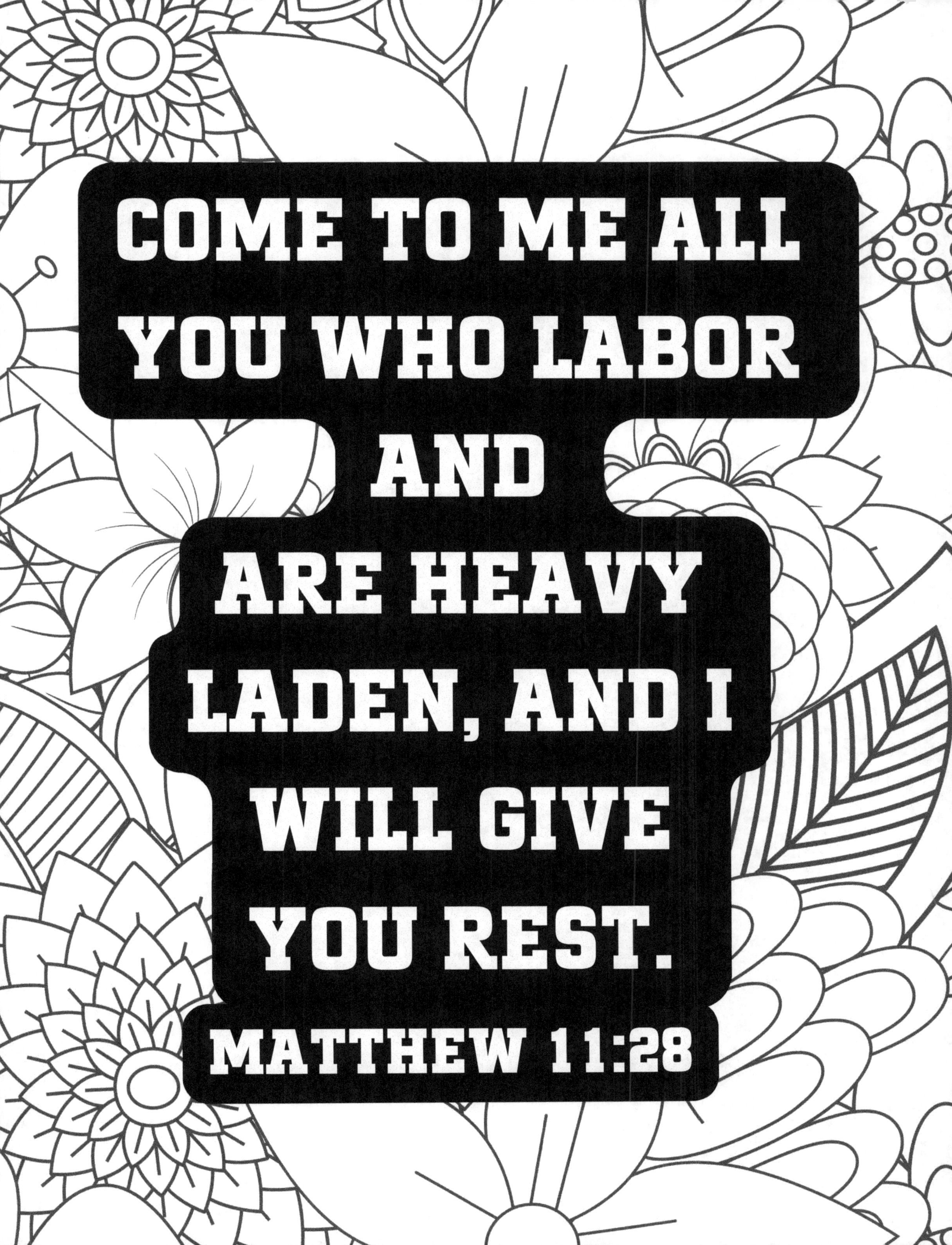

COME TO ME ALL
YOU WHO LABOR
AND
ARE HEAVY
LADEN, AND I
WILL GIVE
YOU REST.
MATTHEW 11:28

DO NOT BE OVERCOME BY EVIL, BUT OVERCOME EVIL WITH GOOD
ROMANS 12:21

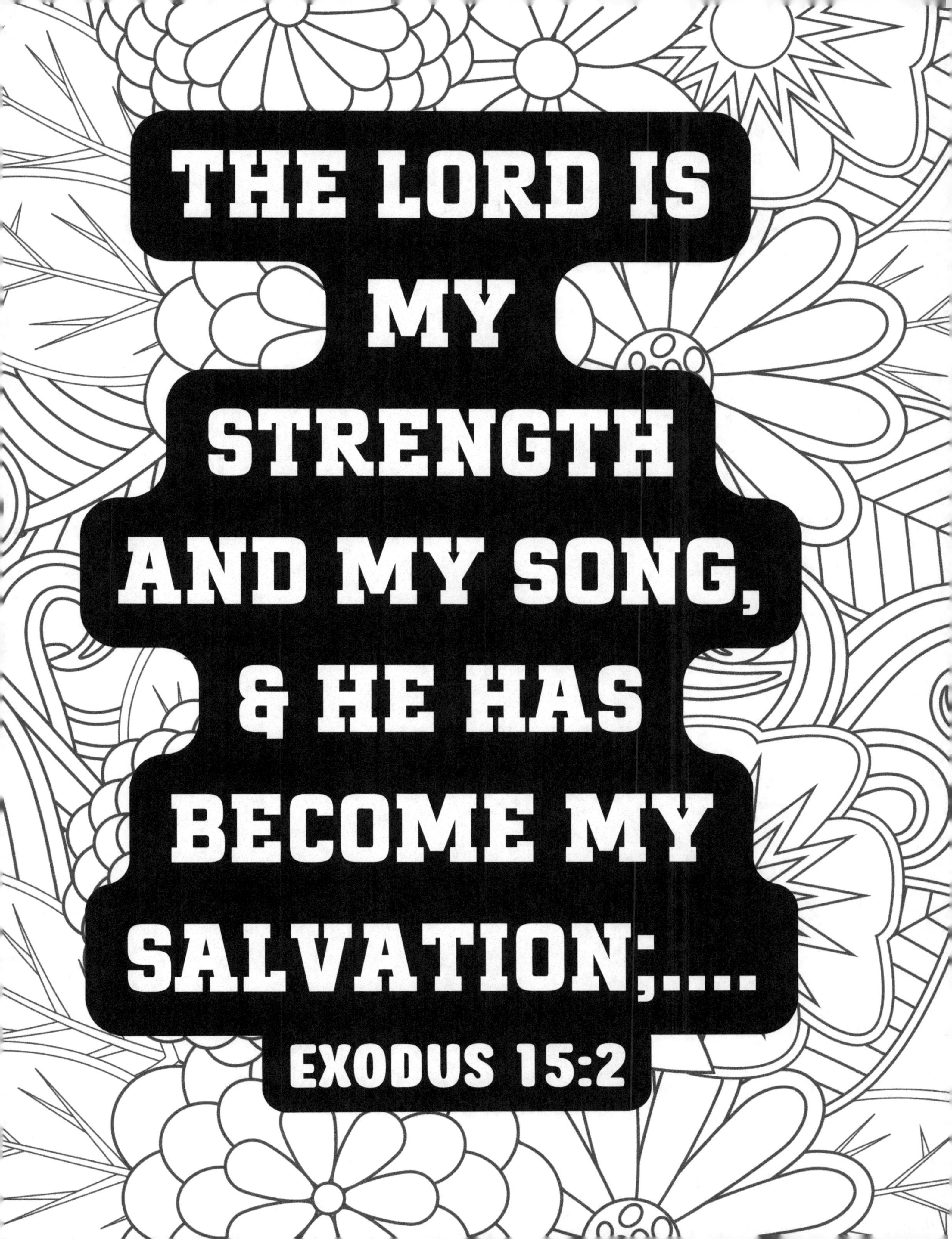

THE LORD IS MY STRENGTH AND MY SONG, & HE HAS BECOME MY SALVATION;....
EXODUS 15:2

DO NOT BE CONFORMED TO THIS WORLD, BUT BE TRANSFORMED BY THE RENEWAL OF YOUR MIND......
ROMANS 12:2

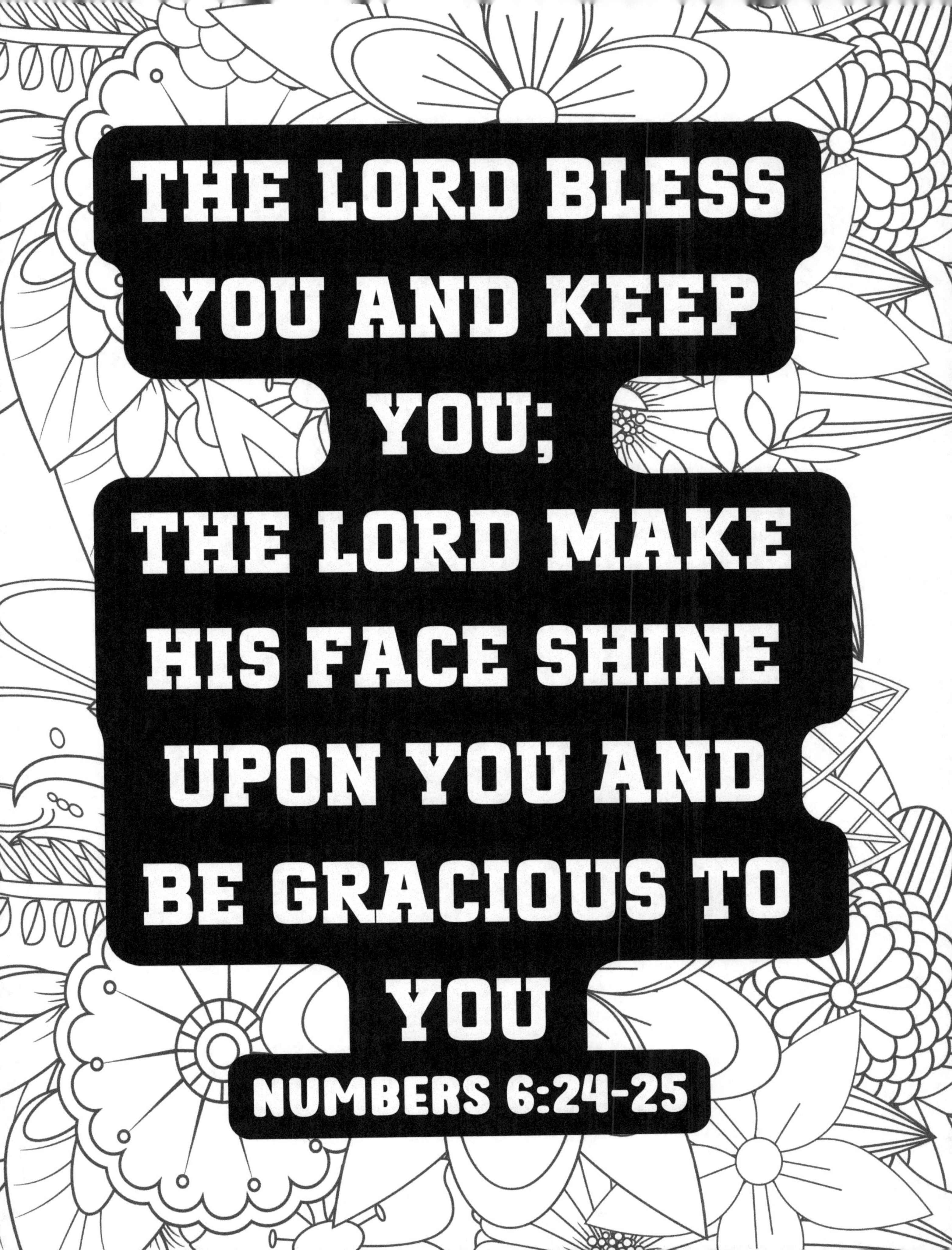

THE LORD BLESS YOU AND KEEP YOU; THE LORD MAKE HIS FACE SHINE UPON YOU AND BE GRACIOUS TO YOU
NUMBERS 6:24-25

REJOICE ALWAYS, PRAY WITHOUT CEASING, GIVE THANKS IN ALL CIRCUMSTANCES, FOR THIS IS THE WILL OF GOD IN CHRIST JESUS

1 THESSALONIANS 5:16-18

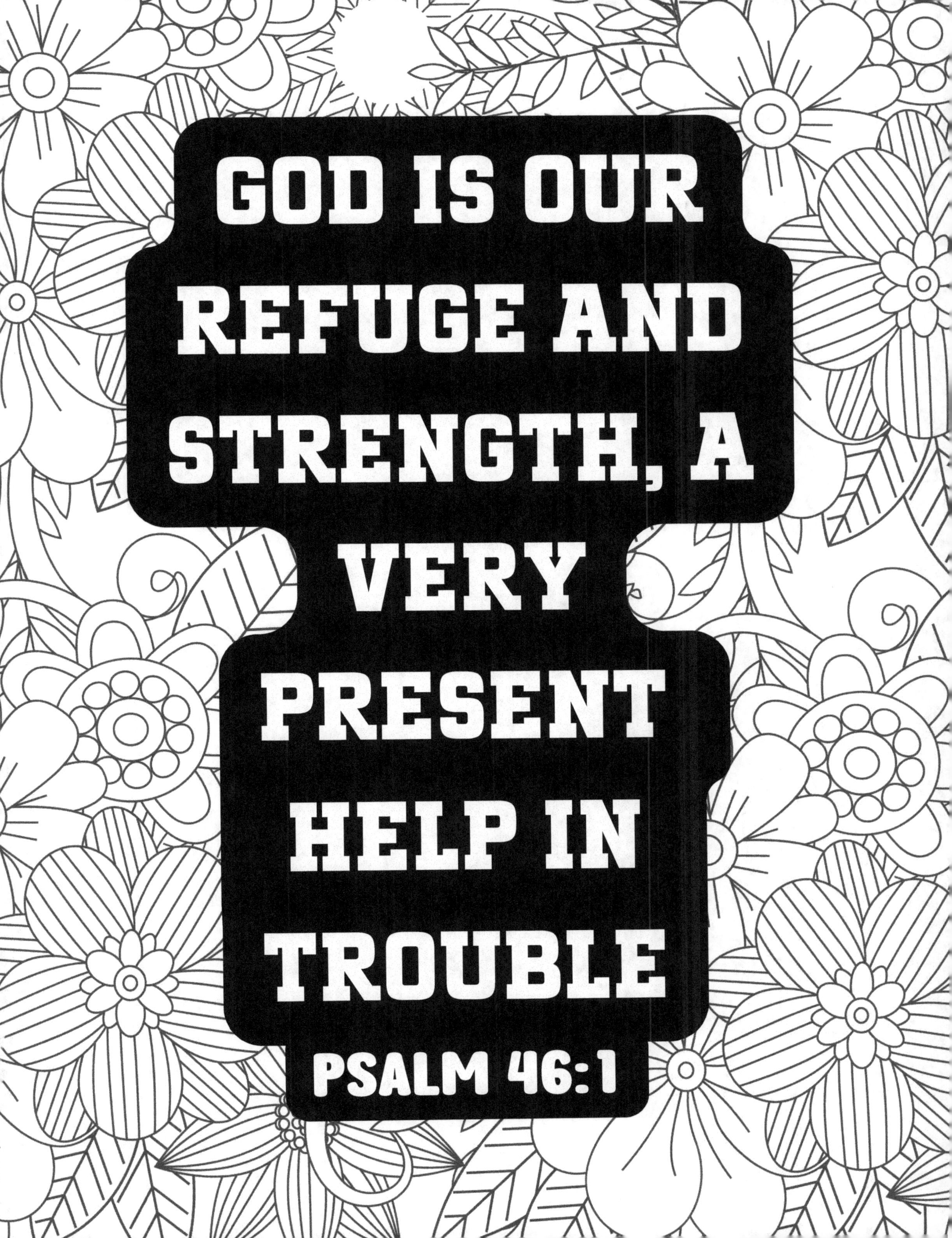

GOD IS OUR REFUGE AND STRENGTH, A VERY PRESENT HELP IN TROUBLE
PSALM 46:1

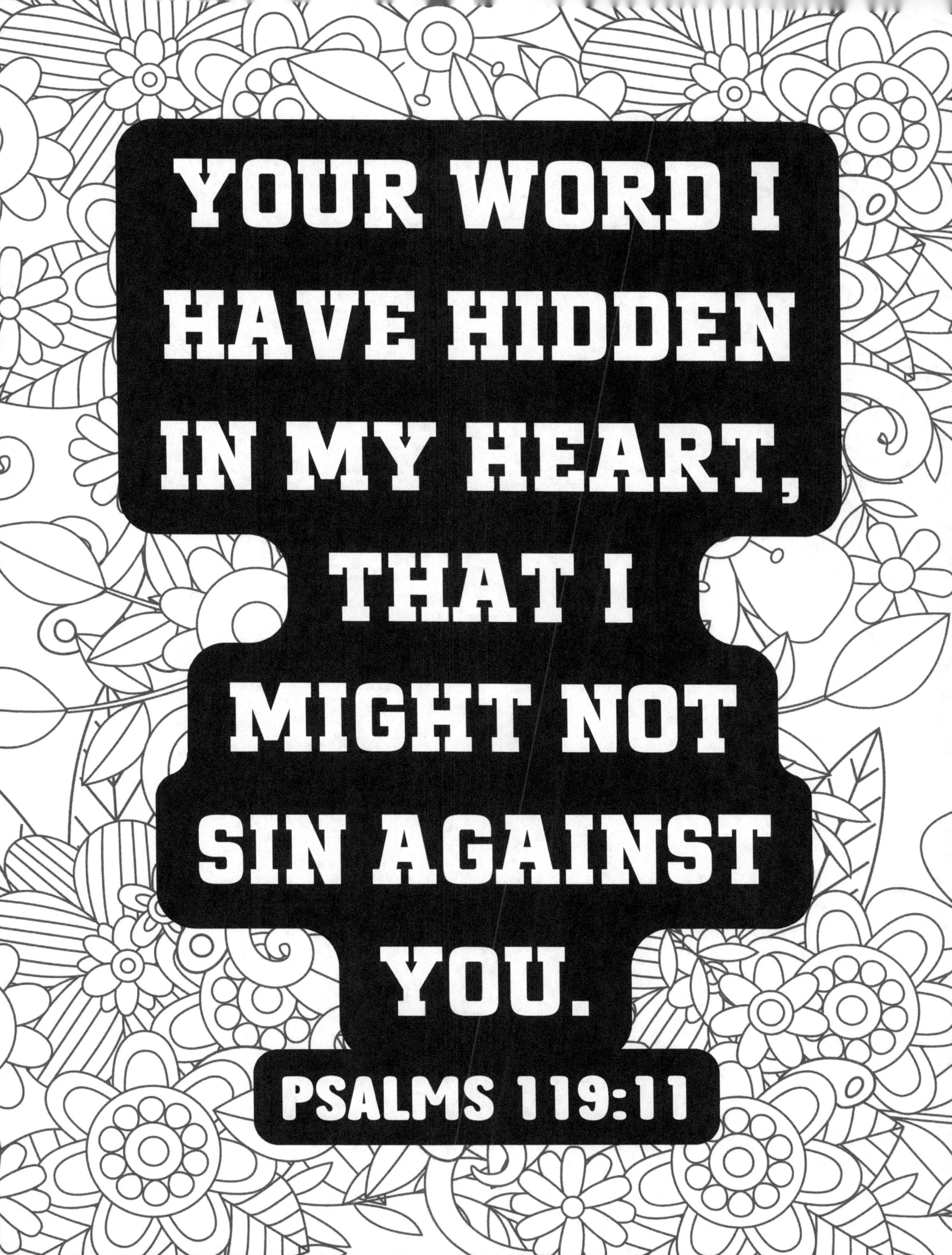
YOUR WORD I HAVE HIDDEN IN MY HEART, THAT I MIGHT NOT SIN AGAINST YOU.
PSALMS 119:11

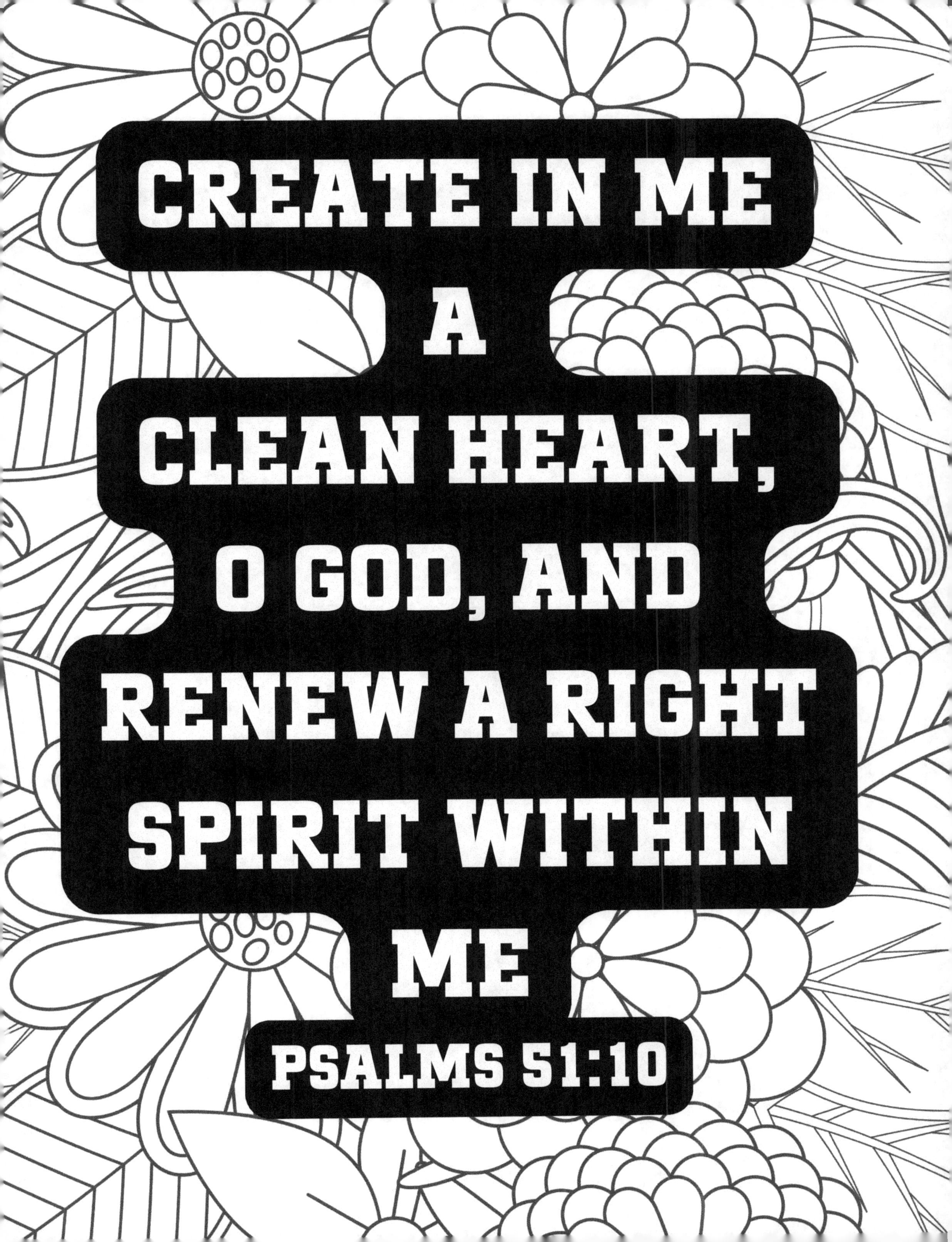
CREATE IN ME A CLEAN HEART, O GOD, AND RENEW A RIGHT SPIRIT WITHIN ME
PSALMS 51:10

LET ALL THAT YOU DO BE DONE IN LOVE
1 CORINTHIANS 16:14

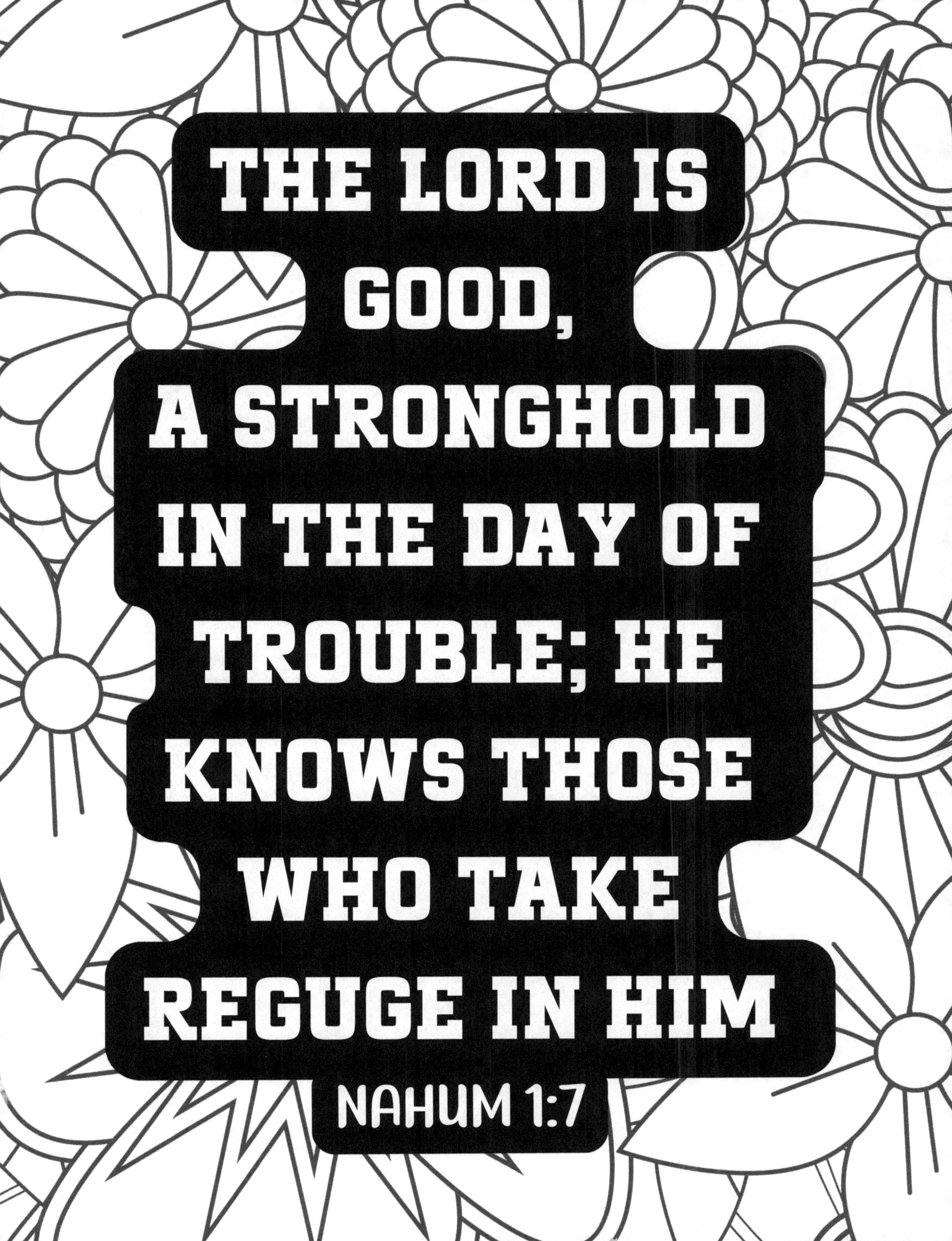

THE LORD IS GOOD,
A STRONGHOLD IN THE DAY OF TROUBLE; HE KNOWS THOSE WHO TAKE REGUGE IN HIM
NAHUM 1:7

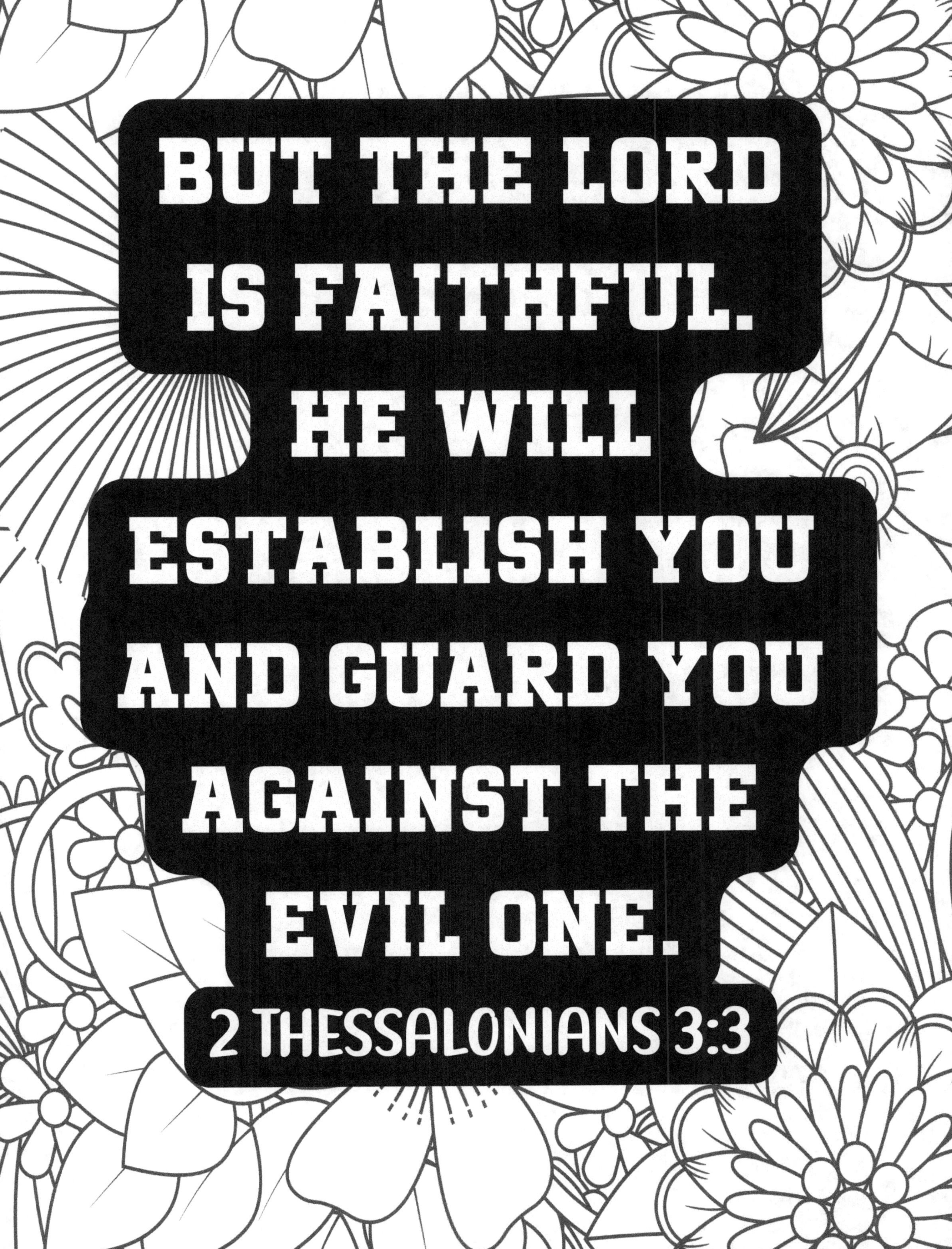

BUT THE LORD IS FAITHFUL.
HE WILL ESTABLISH YOU AND GUARD YOU AGAINST THE EVIL ONE.
2 THESSALONIANS 3:3

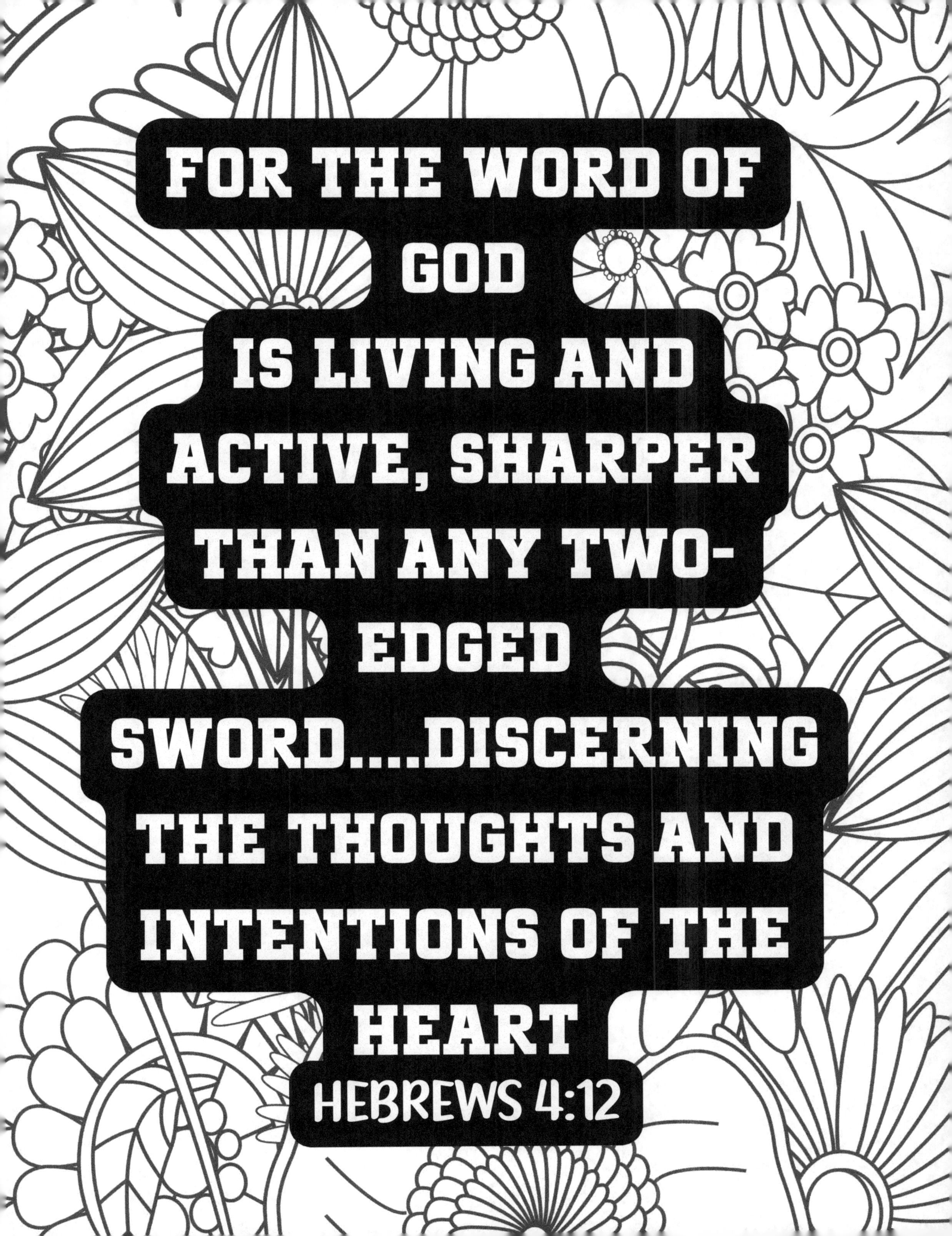

FOR THE WORD OF GOD IS LIVING AND ACTIVE, SHARPER THAN ANY TWO-EDGED SWORD.....DISCERNING THE THOUGHTS AND INTENTIONS OF THE HEART
HEBREWS 4:12

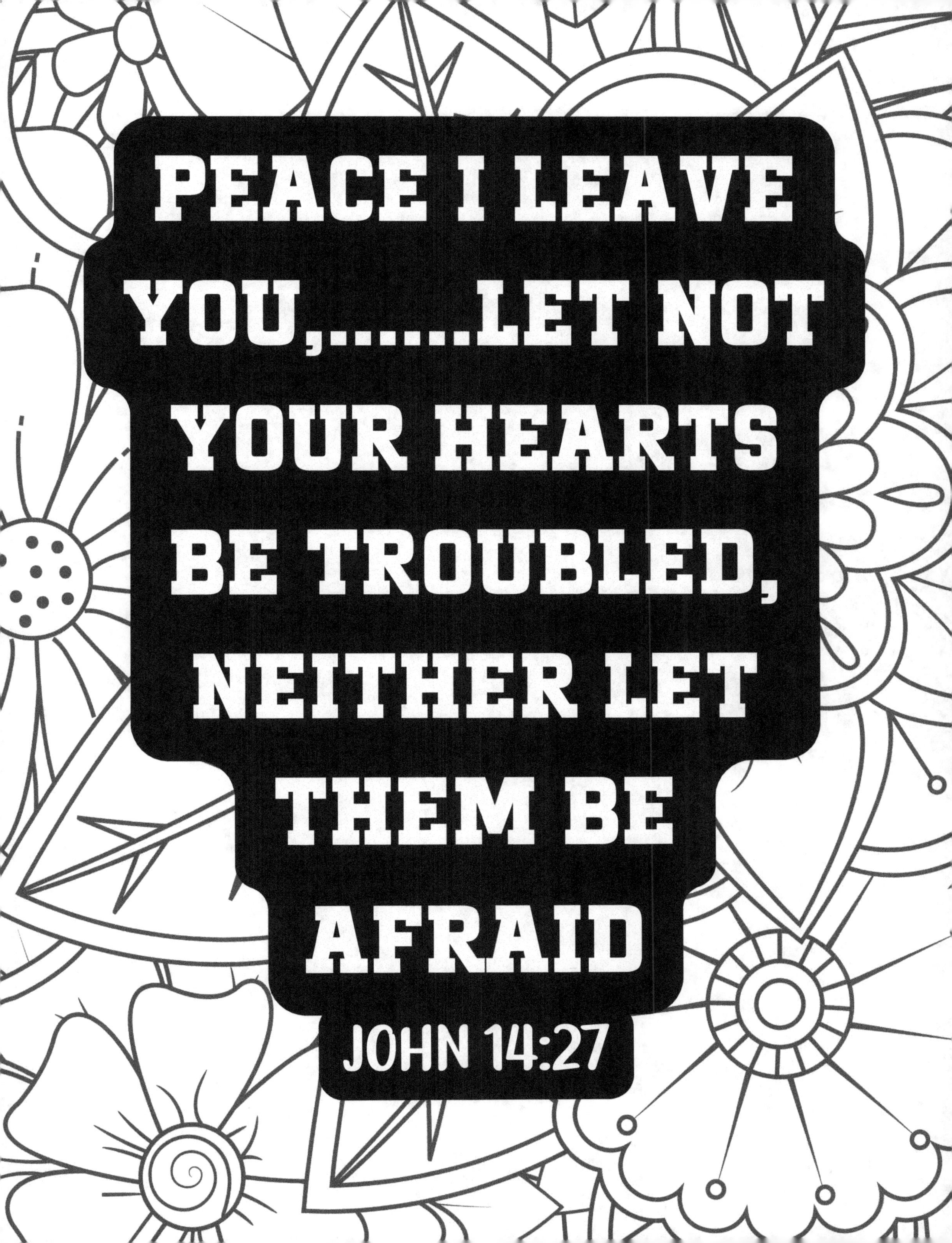

PEACE I LEAVE YOU,......LET NOT YOUR HEARTS BE TROUBLED, NEITHER LET THEM BE AFRAID
JOHN 14:27

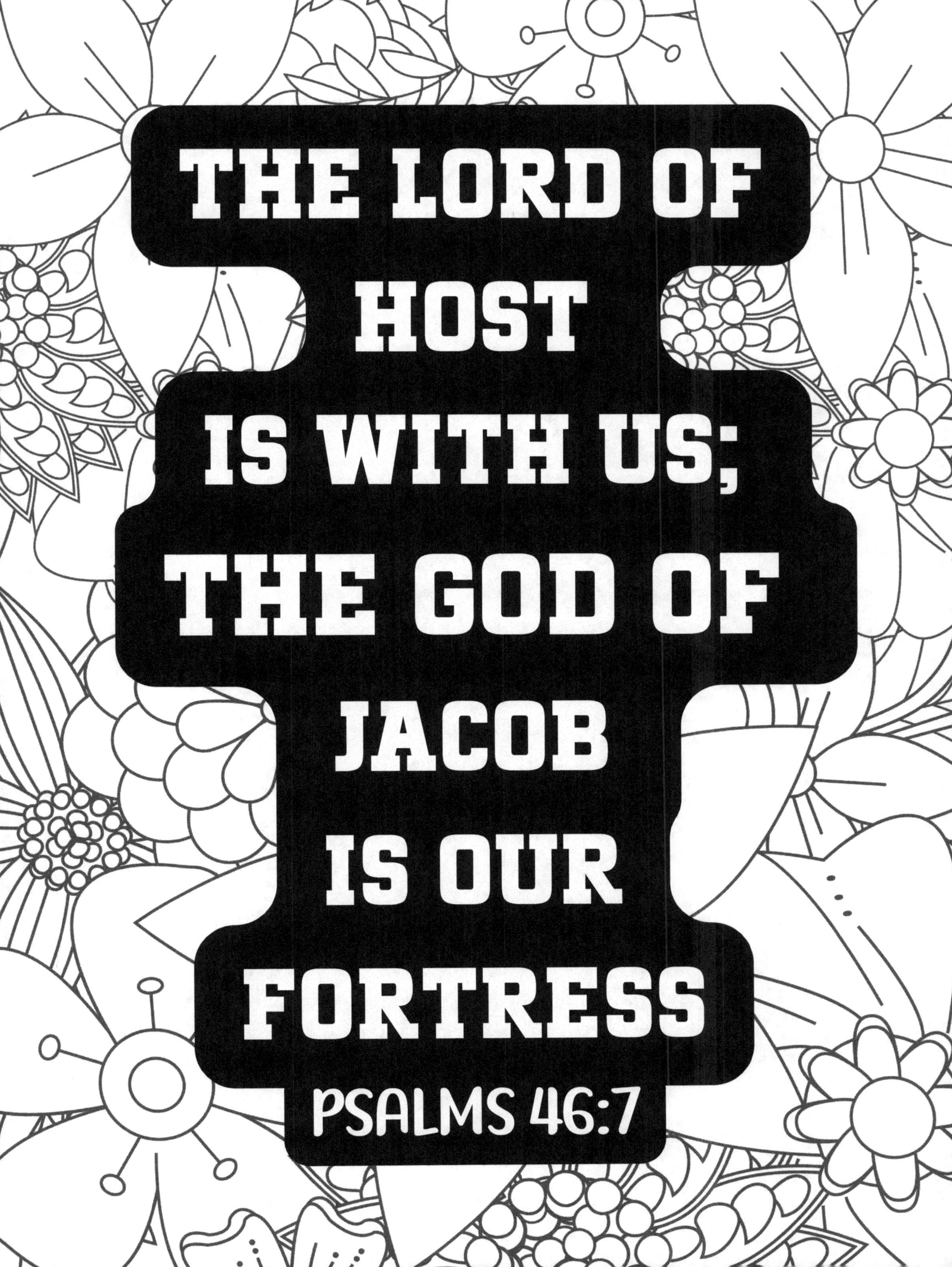
THE LORD OF HOST IS WITH US; THE GOD OF JACOB IS OUR FORTRESS
PSALMS 46:7

BLESSED ARE THE PURE IN HEART, FOR THEY SHALL SEE GOD
MATTHEW 5:8

FOR WHERE YOUR TREASURE IS, THERE YOU HEART WILL BE ALSO
MATTHEW 6:21

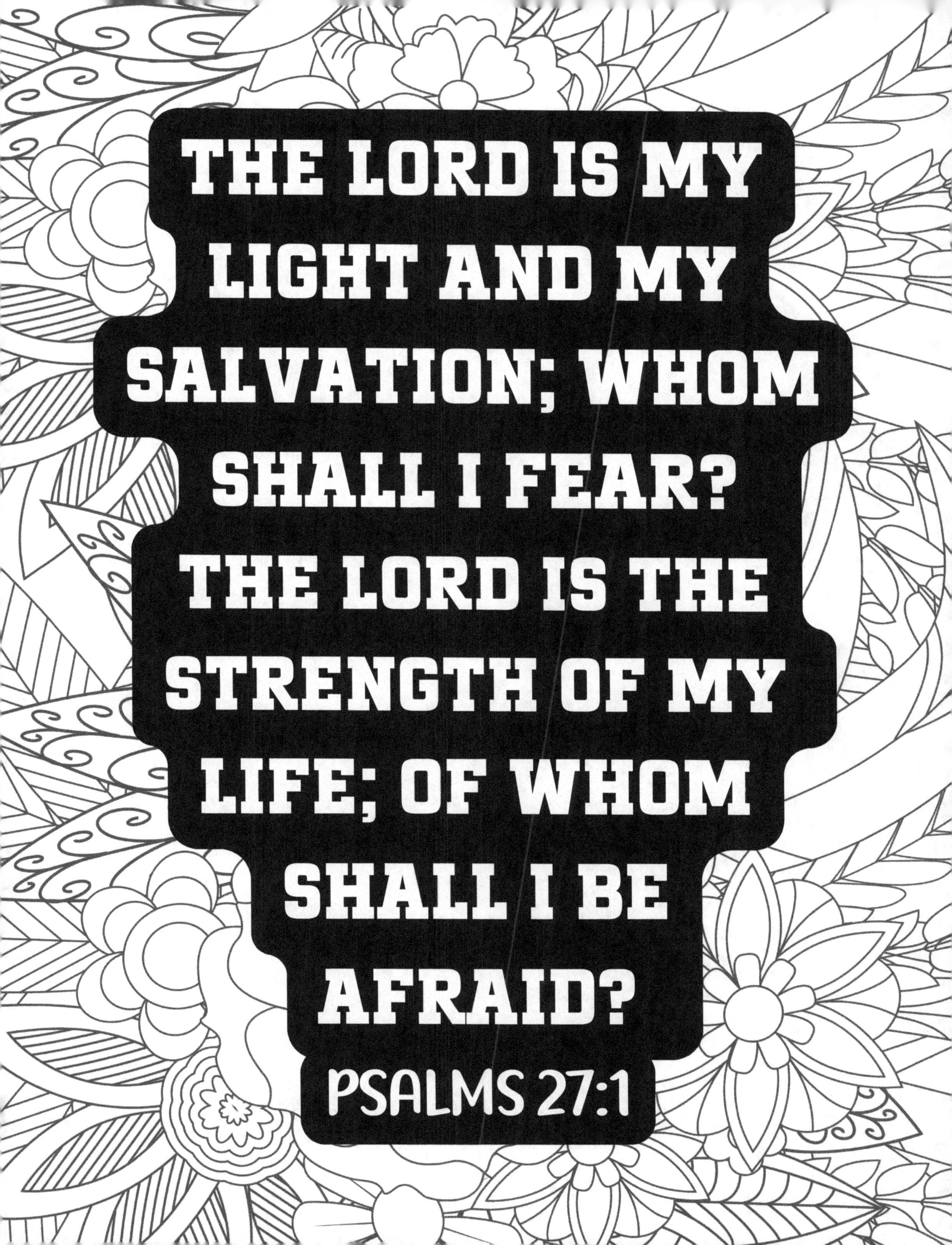

THE LORD IS MY LIGHT AND MY SALVATION; WHOM SHALL I FEAR? THE LORD IS THE STRENGTH OF MY LIFE; OF WHOM SHALL I BE AFRAID?
PSALMS 27:1

SEEK THE LORD AND HIS STRENGTH; SEEK HIS PRESENCE CONTINUALLY
1 CHRONICLES 16:11

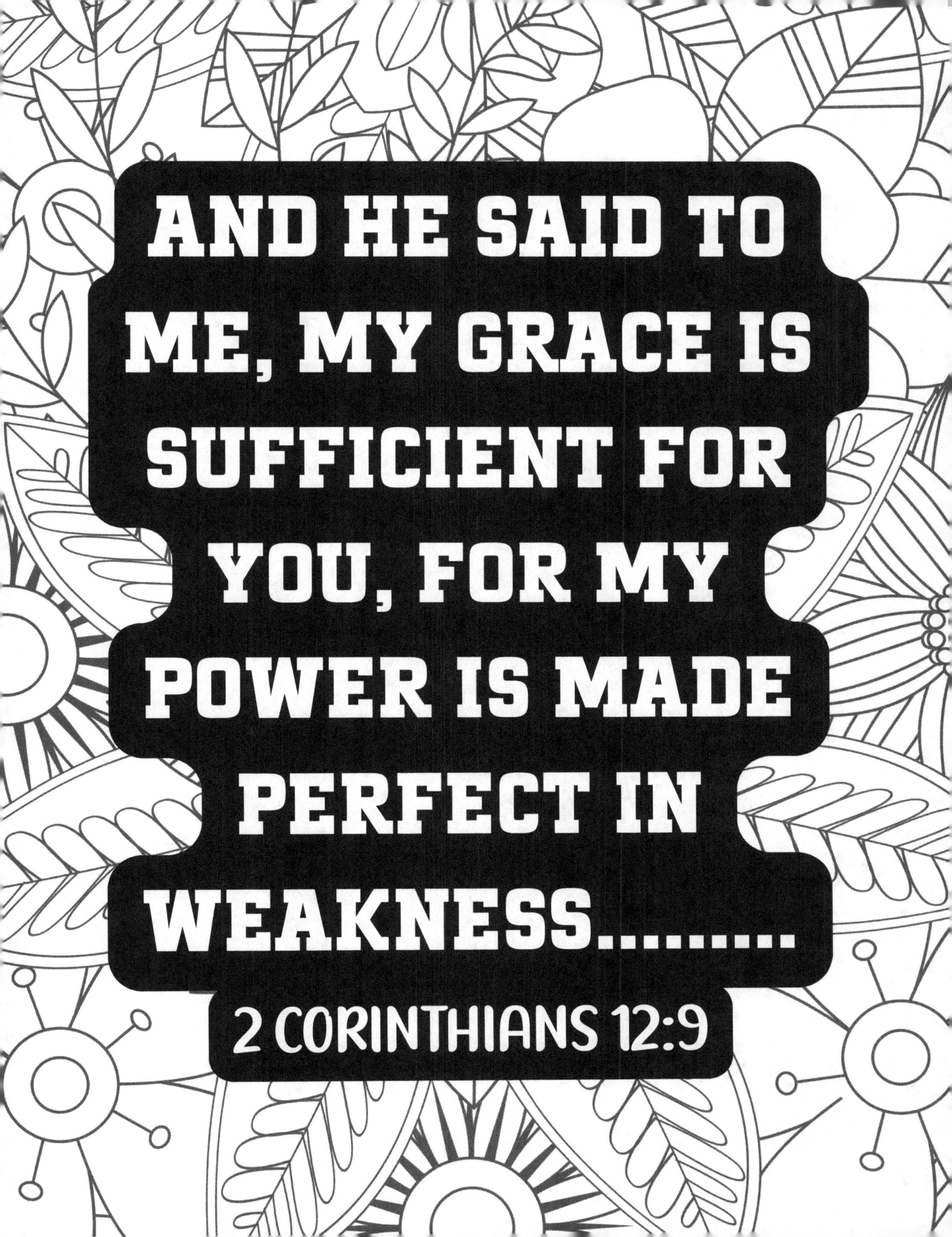

AND HE SAID TO ME, MY GRACE IS SUFFICIENT FOR YOU, FOR MY POWER IS MADE PERFECT IN WEAKNESS..........
2 CORINTHIANS 12:9

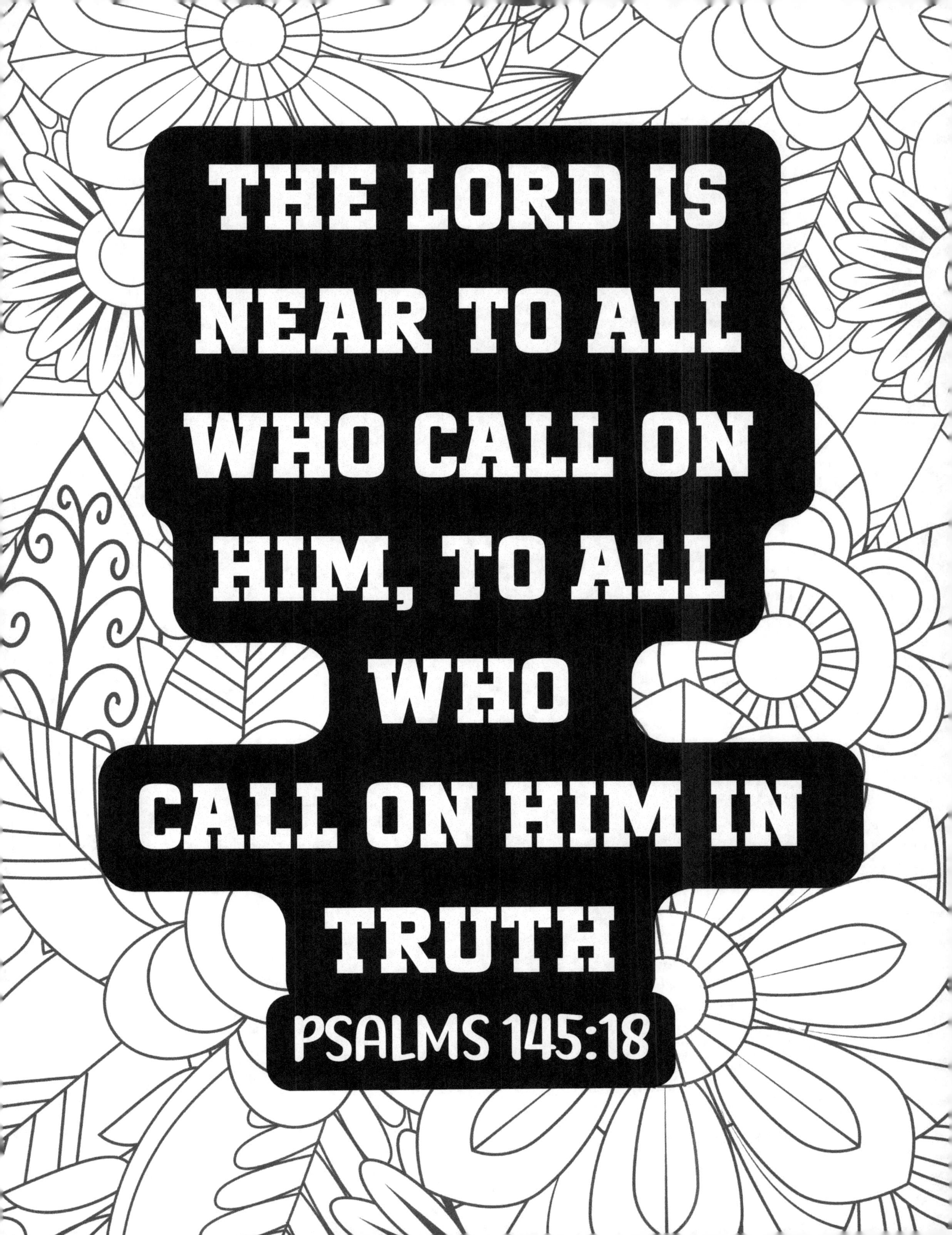

THE LORD IS NEAR TO ALL WHO CALL ON HIM, TO ALL WHO CALL ON HIM IN TRUTH
PSALMS 145:18

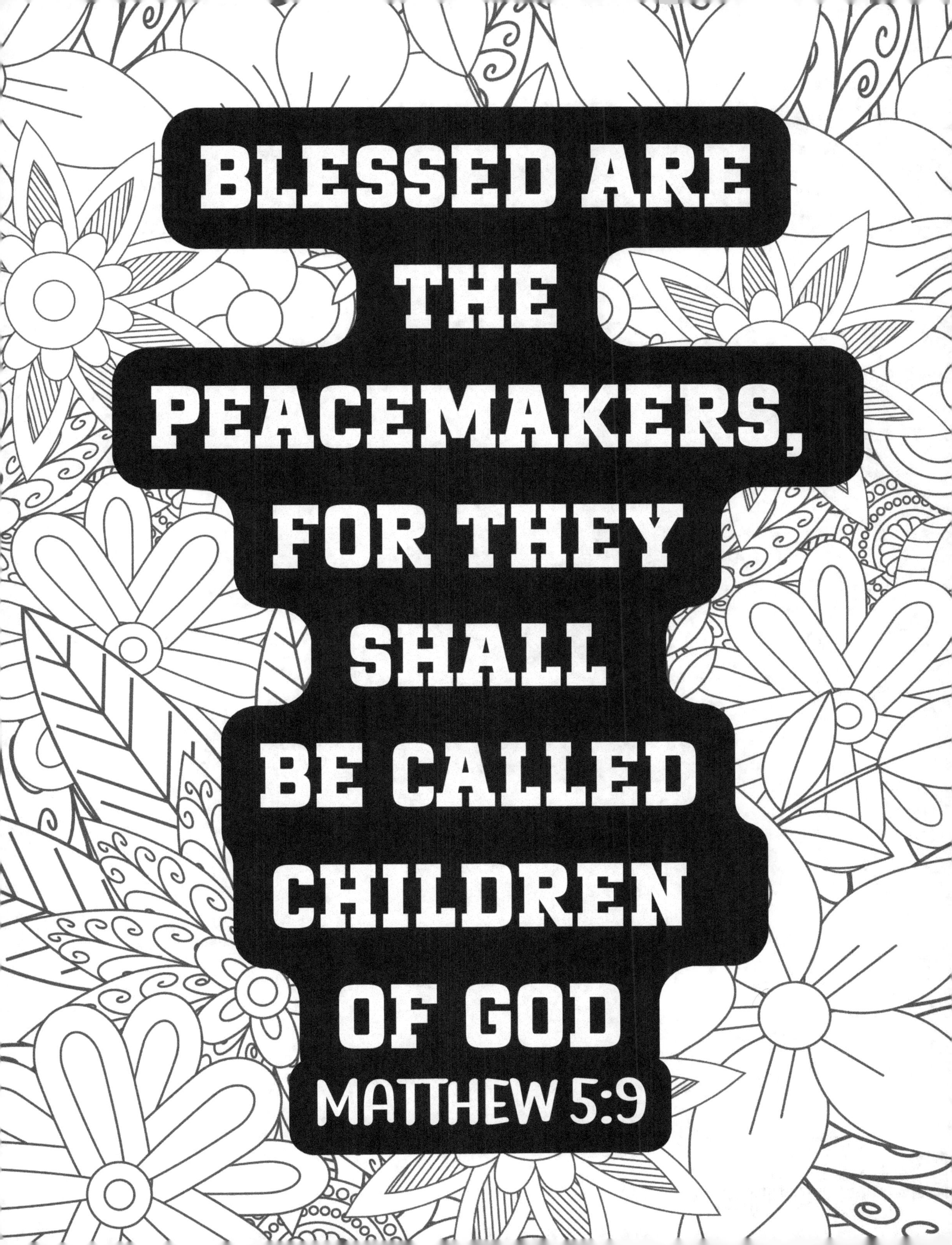

BLESSED ARE THE PEACEMAKERS, FOR THEY SHALL BE CALLED CHILDREN OF GOD
MATTHEW 5:9